Chapters

of the Gospels

James H. Kurt

© 2009, 2021 James H. Kurt. All Rights Reserved.

No part of this book may be reproduced, stored in a retrieval system, or transmitted by any means without the written permission of the author.

Children of Light Publications 1/25/2021
ISBN: 978-1-7332154-9-7

(First published by AuthorHouse 1/12/2009
ISBN: 978-1-4389-3497-6)

Nihil Obstat:
Rev. Donald Blumenfeld
Censor Librorum

Imprimatur:
+ Most Reverend John J. Myers, J.C.D., D.D.
Archbishop of Newark, New Jersey
October 27, 2008

The **Nihil Obstat** and **Imprimatur** are official declarations that a book or pamphlet is free of doctrinal error. No implication is contained therein that those who have granted the **Nihil Obstat** and **Imprimatur** agree with the contents, opinions, or statements expressed.

"It was God who brought forth the mountains of Israel, that is to say, the authors of divine Scriptures. Feed there that you may feed in safety."

St. Augustine, *On Pastors*
(see Liturgy of the Hours, Office of Readings,
Thurs. of the 25th Week in Ord. Time)

Introduction

The title of this work is fairly self-explanatory. In reading the Bible I have noticed that the individual chapters seem to have an organic unity, a movement and meaning of their own. Though we know that chapter and verse were later impositions upon the text of the Word of God, yet this delineation seems itself to be blessed, to bring clarity to the light and logic of the Lord's speaking to us.

Here I pray the Spirit enable me to expose the light in the chapters of the Gospels.

Table of Contents

I. The Gospel of Matthew 1

II. The Gospel of Mark 39

III. The Gospel of Luke 61

IV. The Gospel of John 91

I.

The Gospel of Matthew

Chapter 1 – Conceived of the Spirit

Here the New Testament begins. Here the Word of Truth goes forth now in fullness. May the Spirit move us, and move us well.

On this the feast of St. Jerome, I set out upon this writing. On this day I happen to learn of those who set the Word of God into chapters and into verses, I begin to look upon the chapters of the Gospels one by one, beginning here with the first chapter of St. Matthew.

In this first chapter of the New Testament, we hear initially of the forty-two generations from Abraham to Jesus, our Savior, divided equally into three sections of fourteen.

How perfectly salvation history unfolds in God's hands; how wonderfully He prepares the world for His Son's coming. And what a wonder it is for Him to come into our midst. There is a perfection beyond words about all that God does. And what greater perfection is there than that of His Son?

There are, of course, all manner of men (and women) from whom our Savior descends in His humanity, though none of these is in Him, for He is kept free of the stain of sin of evil kings and prostitutes and murderers... kept apart even from the holiest among us. None of us could father Him who bears all of us, but of us, nonetheless, He willingly becomes. And here we trace His origins, His origins on this earth.

Forever the Son existed in Heaven with the Father, with the Spirit, in eternity, with no beginning or end; but to us He does come, stepping into time with the creatures made through Him. He comes not of human generation, but that regeneration of the human race might be fulfilled, might be brought to light.

And the wonder that is the coming of the Son of Man is too marvelous for the mind of even a good man, one of the righteous sons of the Father of Abraham, Isaac, and Jacob, to comprehend. And so it is in a dream the LORD addresses Joseph; it is through an angel He speaks to the man who would be called the father of His only Son. Mary His Mother is prepared beforehand by God's will, but Joseph must here be convinced that this Child conceived in his betrothed is the One who will save us from our sins.

Matthew

But to wife he takes her; believe in the word that comes to him he does. And it is he who names Him Jesus, the Name the angel imparts.

> O LORD, we thank you that you have saved us,
> that your Son has come to be with sinful man
> and brought us to birth again,
> that in the Spirit we too might be conceived
> and enter the generation of your heavenly kingdom.

Chapter 2 – Blessed Pilgrimage

A chapter of travel, of pilgrimage – of flight from the face of one king and in search of another. To find Him who is the Ruler of Israel and Prince of all hearts, we must flee the presence of the ruler of this age.

To Bethlehem the Magi come, led by the star hailing the rising of the King of the Jews. But through the house of Herod they must pass, through the kingdom of this world their travel takes them – and away from it entirely they must remain, once they have seen the face of our Savior.

Joseph, too, is called to leave the realm of the evil king, bringing the Child and His Mother to the land of Egypt (that place of slavery all must escape). Out of darkness all are called, away from sin and death all are led, that the slaughter of souls might be avoided, that safe haven might be discovered by the glory of God.

The Lord prepares a place for us – heavenly rooms await our souls, yes, but even here He is our refuge, and in Him and His guidance our lodging we make. And though the innocent among us may be slaughtered, though the sound of weeping rise from this valley of tears, yet even those whose blood is shed find their place secure in Him… and the cry of the just is answered.

Pursue us as he will, the prince of this world will never find our souls at his disposal. Protected ever are those who seek the Lord, who follow the light that leads through this world to the presence of the Christ. As futile as any effort to overshadow the Word of God, so futile will be any effort to destroy those who make their home in Him.

Safely in the arms of our Mother we shall rest, the angels watching over our every step.

> O LORD, though the darkness surround us and close in,
> yet your angel comes to guide us.
> As Joseph carried your Son and His Mother
> to the places reserved by you,
> so lead us on right paths each day –
> till we enter your house and see your face.

Chapter 3 – The Voice Crying Out

The voice crying out in the wilderness. The Baptist preparing the way of the Lord. With water he washes repentant souls clean of their sins. But the fire of the Spirit is on the horizon.

Yes, the ax lies at the root of the trees. All unable to stand before the Son in His day will be cut to the ground and thrown into the fire. Indeed, all shall know the fire the Lord Jesus brings – some for purification and renewal to everlasting life, others for eternal condemnation. There is no escaping the fire of the Lord. Thus does John seek to prepare our souls.

And the words of the one whom the prophet foretold do not shy the least from the truth. If he should swallow his words the fire would consume him where he stands. As it is, he is not afraid to shout out the sins of any man; his heart is fixed firmly on calling all to saving repentance. His is a love that will not abide any fawning pretense.

For the winnowing fan is indeed in the hand of the Lord. The end is upon us now. Jesus Christ enters the scene, a marvel beyond human capacity to understand. And so long as we wallow in our sins, the Lord's grace will never penetrate our dissipated souls, but our hearts will rot where we stand.

Jesus comes, and He is baptized. He places Himself under John's hand. And as the water envelops Him, new life comes to the cesspool that is our domain. And the Spirit Himself cannot help but become manifest; and the Father Himself must speak – for here indeed is the Beloved Son, and fallen humanity now enters on the path of

Matthew

redemption... a path God the Father, Son, and Holy Spirit would but see come to fruition.

Alleluia! we must sing, the Spirit of God alighting upon us now. Listen, my brother, my sister, to the voice of John – the call to reformation does yet go forth, and only in heeding this powerful word will we come to please our God.

> O Jesus, Savior, send your Spirit now upon our souls;
> let your fire redeem us from all paths of evil.
> Ready let us be to heed the word of John,
> that with you we may rest in the Father's arms.

Chapter 4 – Light Arises

Light has arisen. The devil is cast out, darkness is banished, and the dawn that is the Son begins to cover the earth with God's Light.

The devil and his devious plots fail to conquer the unconquerable Lord; by the word of Scripture, Satan is defeated, and he must flee the sight of the Father's glory reflected in this His Son. Though Jesus be subjected to the frailty of the flesh, to the weakness of its needs, yet He finds strength in fidelity to the commands of God. And His Father is with Him; and His angels minister to Him... and the devil is left speechless by the Word come forth from our Savior's mouth.

And to the land of darkness Jesus does now come. Satan holding no sway, He can readily cast out any disease, every frailty by which we were wont to fall. To restore the image of our Creator He has come; and Christ, the Image of God, His disciples recognize as they look up from their nets to the Man standing upon the shore. The water itself finds joy in kissing His feet, as with hearts aflame the fishermen brothers leave all to follow Him.

Yes, all come. All of faith seeking healing from the darkness of sin eating away at body and soul follow Him in great numbers, and none is disappointed: in this Light they find their home, they see their redemption won. But now it begins; here on the shores of Galilee the dawn first appears, particularly to the eyes of Peter and Andrew and James and John. For these will follow not only for healing, but to be healers themselves of all who hear the word Jesus declares: "Repent, for the kingdom of heaven is at hand."

Reach out and touch Him, my brothers and sisters. Let the devil hold no sway over your soul. Setting aside all lust for power and money (for vainglory upon this plane) and worshiping the LORD in obedience to His commands, reach out to His Son and to His apostles… and you too will be drawn into the kingdom of God.

> Your light has come, O Lord.
> You endure temptation for our sake,
> that we might conquer it in your Name.
> No death in sight, or in our hearts or minds,
> let us follow you now along this shoreline.

Chapter 5 – The Call to Perfection

The Sermon on the Mount and the call to perfection – to reflect the glory of our heavenly Father. Nothing short of such perfection will enter the kingdom of God.

From His seat upon the mountain, Jesus imparts His vision of heaven. His eyes see all and His word is truth, and the light that fills Him He would share with others.

What do the eyes of Jesus see as He looks out upon the world? He sees anger, He sees strife… He sees a merciless pride and a lust of the heart that poisons man's very existence. And He knows this cannot be. He knows that none of this is present in His Father's House; and so any who would enter there must be purged of all such sin, or be cast into Gehenna.

And so His words are clear, of light itself, and cannot be denied, cannot be gainsaid by any mind – for the mind of Christ is blind to no matter, while the mind of man sees little that is not darkened by sin.

When the Lord looks out upon His disciples, He sees also those who mourn, those who hunger for righteousness… those whose hearts are broken by persecution but continue to strive for the great blessing that is theirs in Him who now looks upon them. And He is comforted. And He would encourage them. He does not tell them to take their ease but challenges them to enter further through the narrow

Matthew

gate, that their blessing might increase – that they might indeed share completely in His light.

Let His word be brought to perfection in us, brothers and sisters. Let us find our thirst slaked by following in His way, the way of the Cross, the way of truth. Let our righteousness surpass that of the scribes and Pharisees (and all those who would shorten the arm of the Lord) that it might reflect God's own.

What joy we should find in our Savior's exhortation to leave behind all measure of anger and lust that we might know His love in its fullness. To be perfect as our heavenly Father is perfect! What greater call can there be than this?

And so, remain in peace with your brother, love your wife, accept the persecution of an unjust world even as a blessing of God, as an opportunity to show your love as strong as your Lord, the Christ… and in His love you will indeed share, His glory you will indeed know – nothing but light will fill your soul, and so your spirit will enter the realm of heaven.

> The letter of your law let us follow, O Lord;
> perfection let us find in walking with you.
> For your law is love, love of all –
> let not even death turn us from your way.
> In the kingdom of heaven let us make our home,
> even on this corrupted plane.

Chapter 6 – Treasure in Heaven

Do not seek the things of this world, nor the praise of this world in doing the things of God. Let your treasure be in heaven; there let your heart rest.

The Lord would not have us concerned for the things of this earth, for He knows how passing these things are and that they are not difficult to attain for one who sets His heart on God. As His Sermon continues, He teaches us of the dichotomy between the kingdom of heaven and that of the world – between serving God and mammon – and the attitude we must possess toward all we have and all we do.

Chapters of the Gospels

To rise above matters regarding the things of this world is necessary, certainly, for these should matter to us not at all. Whether we are rich or poor, what is that? Whether we eat or drink or dress well... of what concern are the things of the body to us? We take our life in the Spirit and not the flesh, and so no attention, no worry, should we pay to what is of the flesh.

But even in heavenly things, even in the practice of prayer and almsgiving, even in fasting, we must beware not to possess such gifts as things to be bought and sold – as opportunity for power or prestige. We must do heavenly things with a heavenly attitude, which dispossesses us of any pride in these things, or still we will be serving not God but mammon, and our religion will be quite vain.

All must be done without expecting return from the world; all must be done for God alone. Let it be Him who sees us, who knows us, Him whom we desire to please, and true reward will come to us; for then we will be as His sons.

Do you know the secret place of which our Savior speaks? Are you familiar with the hidden acts done in God's sight? Do you quietly offer your sacrifice? Or is your prayer but for others' ears, your alms given for the praise of men, and your fasting done that they might look with pity on your soul?

Let the kingdom of the Lord come into your lives. Let go of all things that blind your eyes to your nothingness and our good God's omnipotence. If you know of His gentle care for even the weakest among us, if you recognize His blessing upon all that lives and breathes, what could trouble you, my brother? For then you would know how much He loves you and watches over you.

Put all in His hands and your light will shine without disturbance; your eye will be whole and you will be as He is. Then your prayers will be truly fruitful, and all you offer will be acceptable to Him.

> O Lord, into your heavenly kingdom let us come this day.
> Your blessed creatures let us ever be.
> You see and know our hearts, O Lord;
> let them be pure and serve your holy will,
> that no thief may break in and destroy.

Chapter 7 – On Bearing Fruit

Jesus finishes His astonishing teaching on the mountain. With authority He speaks. Let us listen to His words – and let us act on them.

By our fruits we will be judged; if we bear good fruit we will stand strong on His day, but if our tree is rotten and our fruit corrupted, what awaits us but the fire? Our house shall collapse when come the winds and rain.

We may attempt to fool ourselves but, again (and always), the Lord looks upon our heart and He knows all our ways. The judgment, the unholy leaven that poisons our soul, He sees in the light of His presence. It is indeed as a wooden beam in our eye, blinding us regarding all we do and making all we do quite worthless. It will cause us only to be trampled underfoot.

But if we wish with genuine hearts to follow and serve the Lord our God, then all such foolishness we must put aside and walk the narrow path to heaven. (How shall our swollen heads pass through the straitened gates otherwise?)

Ask the Lord and He will give you strength, and He will give you guidance. Beg your Father; He will not deny any good petition of His children. If truly you desire His love and His life, then listen for His answer, set your soul upon His words, and do what He bids you.

He wishes you to love Him, yes, and to love your brother. He desires your obedient response, and so to work in His garden. He would see you a fruitful tree and a tender of those shoots around you. None would He have destroyed, but all come into His kingdom.

But we must listen to the Son's words of truth, and do the Father's blessed will.

> O Lord, how shall I stand on your holy day,
> I who am so filled with judgment?
> How shall I find your perfect way,
> who am so deaf to your commandments?
> Help me to grow as a tree blessed by you –
> setting aside all the evil in me,
> let me come to dwell in your kingdom.

Chapters of the Gospels

Chapter 8 – The Power of His Word

O the power that goes forth from the Son of God! By a word He heals; by a word He casts out demons... by a word He calms the winds and the waves. Is nothing impossible for Him?

Jesus now comes down from the mountain, and the power of His teaching, of His word, now becomes evident. Principally we find a series of healings in this chapter, as the crowds follow closely our Savior's tracks. But who indeed will have faith to follow where He leads?

The centurion exhibits great faith. This commander of men understands the power of a word, and he believes that the Lord possesses that power to the greatest degree. He believes that by a word from Jesus' mouth his servant will be healed. He needs no further proof of the Lord's power. And the servant is thus healed. The centurion goes in absolute faith that the work is done, and it is so. Yes, it is so.

And what faith the leper shows, on his knees before Jesus declaring, "If you wish, you can make me clean." And his faith saves him. And he is made well. (The Savior's touch upon his skin he invites by his humble petition.)

And Peter's mother-in-law rises at His touch. And at His word: "Go then!" the spirits leave the demoniacs. He cures all the sick by a word from His mouth.

But will *we* have the faith to follow Him to the other side? Are we able to leave all behind and so embody the conviction needed to arrive at the kingdom of God? Or do we fear the wind and the sea as do the disciples, thinking that on the way we might lose our lives? Renewal, salvation... the far shore of heaven we shall only find by having no place in this world to rest our heads. For as long as we are satisfied with things as they are, as long as we believe nothing can change our lives or save us from distress or oppression, so long will we remain mired in sin – as hopeless as any leprous man.

Do not drive the Lord from your province. Do not fear His power at work in your house. If you hold to the swine that wallow in the swill of this forsaken land, the land of heaven and the bread of angels you shall never know. All things of this earth, polluted as it is, must be left aside as you travel with Him across the sea. And your boat shall be moored in safe harbor. And you too will be healed and made clean, however great your sins may be.

> O Lord, you are our salvation;
> you are our healing.
> By your word, by your touch,
> you make us whole in the sight of God.
> Let us but have faith in you.

<u>Chapter 9</u> – Saving Faith

The healings continue, and great ones at that, as the Lord's power is matched by the faith of those in need. Yet now we begin to hear the objections raised, the questions and doubts that will lead inevitably to His death.

Jesus heals the blind and the mute, as well as the woman with the hemorrhage. He raises the paralytic and the dead, moved with pity for all who are troubled, all in need. And in each case He is inspired by their faith.

The people carry the paralytic to Jesus on a stretcher, knowing where their help lies. The official kneels at His feet, declaring He can raise his daughter who has died. The woman makes her way through the crowd just to touch the tassel of His cloak (and her bleeding is stopped). And the blind men stand before our Savior saying they do believe He can cure them. Faith is all that will save us.

But the murmurings do here begin. Who is He that forgives sin? "This man is blaspheming." "Why does [He] eat with tax collectors and sinners?" And why is it His "disciples do not fast?" For each of these doubts Jesus has answer: "The Son of Man has authority on earth to forgive sins"; "I did not come to call the righteous but sinners"; and, "People do not pour new wine into old wineskins." But who will hear His wisdom and believe in His authority? Who will come to know He is the Son of God?

The crowds rejoice for the wonders performed before their eyes; struck with awe, they glorify God for His power at work among them. Those who thirst cannot but give thanks that their cries are now being answered. But what of those who "harbor evil thoughts," who are not pleased with the graces He displays, the power that is greater than their own? They say, "He drives out demons by the prince of demons"; they begin their call for His crucifixion.

It is only by faith that any are saved, and those without faith may go even so far as to call that which is good evil. Then who can save them from condemnation? How shall their souls be healed? Their only hope has become a cause for cursing.

He is the Son of David; He is the Son of God, the Bridegroom whose new wine must be poured into new wineskins. But if our skins are not prepared, if our hearts reject that which is meant for our salvation, what can we be but burst asunder?

None is dead to Him, but only sleeping. Do not ridicule His word or deny His power, or your disease will remain with you and only grow worse… until your death is permanent.

> O Lord, we are "like sheep without a shepherd";
> have pity on our poor souls.
> Reveal your power at work in our midst –
> send forth laborers into your harvest
> to teach and to heal, to proclaim your saving Gospel.

Chapter 10 – The Commissioning

Jesus commissions His twelve apostles, sending them out as sheep in the midst of wolves, calling them to lose their lives for His sake, letting them know they will be hated by the world because they come in His Name.

This chapter is constituted almost exclusively of the Lord's words of instruction to His disciples. First we are introduced to the Twelve; then Jesus is quoted for the remaining verses. And what teaching is here, set down not only for the Twelve to hear, but for all the disciples who follow in their wake. Jesus is sent by the Father, He sends forth the Twelve, and all share in their mission work who give their descendants even a cup of cold water. Here the vine begins to branch out, and to the ends of the earth it extends.

And what bitter fruit our Savior calls us to drink, a wine none other than He Himself partakes upon the Cross. As He states, "If they have called the master of the house Beelzebul, how much more those of His household!" Thus, we of His household must be prepared to endure even mortal wounds inflicted in opposition to His Name.

And there is no choice in this, brothers and sisters. There is no other path to heaven than that of persecution. As Jesus was, as were His apostles, so must we be: sharing in the sacrifice that is our Savior's call. Severe indeed is the way we must walk.

Yet the Lord our God is with us on this narrow path. He has walked the way before our feet were formed, and He knows and walks with us in all our tribulation, thus making light even the heaviest burden. His eyes see each hair upon our head; nothing escapes His vision – and He will justify all faithful souls when the end has come.

So fear not the cost of your discipleship. The price you must pay is a pittance compared to the glory that awaits you. And though you must turn even from members of your own family, though you must lay down even your own life… there is a life much greater than this one we see, both for you and for the members of your household. To come to heaven and bring others there should be your abiding concern.

And so, let us go forth with the Lord's disciples, healing the sick and driving out demons. Let us not be afraid to speak His words even in hostile places. Peace awaits beyond this time of division. Love we maintain ever in our hearts. For God who is love is with us, and though the apostles be martyred for their faith and for their work, yet eternal bliss is with their immortal souls – and to the heavenly kingdom His sparrows are drawn.

> We love you, O Lord our God,
> and we give our lives for you and your mission.
> For of what worth are we apart from you,
> and what greater gift can we know
> than to give all to you.
> Let us join in your holy sacrifice
> and so be truly blessed.

Chapters of the Gospels
Chapter 11 – The Baptist's Question

The shadow of John the Baptist, chained in Herod's prison, hovers over this entire chapter. Though he himself does not appear, his question and his incarcerated presence inspire all the Lord's teaching here.

When Jesus hears the question John sends through his disciples – "Are you the One who is to come?" – He is touched by the deepest pity, the most profound sympathy. He gives the disciples a simple message in return: See what is done, and do not doubt… quietly, lovingly seeking to reassure the soul who has paved His way. But He cannot help but cry inside for the suffering His children must endure.

As John's disciples leave, our Lord immediately witnesses to the greatness of the Baptist's call. Indeed, he is the greatest of men born of women. Jesus goes so far as to state directly that "he is Elijah," the greatest of prophets, and "more than a prophet" – the messenger of the Lord. He thus reassures Himself as well as the people that here is no "reed swayed by the wind," that despite the fears inherent in his question, there is no man beside him.

Yet John does ask the question. And so Jesus' statement that "the least in the kingdom of heaven is greater than he"; for while we toil upon this plane (and especially so in this time before the Spirit's descent), imperfections remain. In heaven exists no question.

And the plight of John, the intensity of suffering that has broken, at least in part, even this strongest of men, moves the Lord to turn His sights upon those souls surrounding Him. And He fears for their lives. How indeed shall *they* stand?

The reproaches from His mouth are thus severe, chastising those who do not listen, those who do not see – those even where "His mighty deeds had been done," and where His great work has seemingly been in vain. John is enclosed in the darkness of Herod's dungeon; Jesus moves step by step to His crucifixion… yet none repent at the signs they witness – woe to those souls who waste His mission!

The Lord cries out to save them (and us) from the nether world, from ignorance to His truth and His call. The kingdom is suffering violence, the time has come for repentance… and they simply take their ease. What shall save such as these? Not even Sodom has a fate worse than the soul blind to the presence of Christ before his eyes.

Yet at the same time Jesus offers praise to the Father for those who *do* see, to whom the kingdom has been revealed – in all its difficulty – and who have accepted with a whole heart its message, its call, and so are led to the Father by the Son.

These Jesus would hold in His arms. Though they carry the burden of John, though their cross approach our Savior's own… accepting His gentle yoke upon themselves, having faith that this *is* the Savior who has come – He would give rest to such faithful souls, for He would take their burden upon Himself and set them free from all anxiety.

> O Lord, as high as your heavenly power,
> so deep is your sympathy for man.
> All men are reassured by you
> and your gracious presence.
> The violence that overtakes us, let us not fear,
> nor let it take our hearts from you –
> your Cross be our comfort in this life.

Chapter 12 – Lord of the Sabbath

Jesus begins to reveal more clearly who He is. In no uncertain terms He states that He is "greater than Jonah," "greater than Solomon," and "greater than the temple." "The Son of Man is Lord of the Sabbath," with power over even the laws that govern Israel, the laws given to Moses and held by men. For He is all good, and goodness is of God, and goodness is God, and all other things are but His creation – these are good in themselves, but only He has absolute power.

This is the message that must be driven home, not only to the Pharisees and the keepers of the law, but to all souls: Jesus is God. The Spirit of God is upon Him and He accomplishes the will of the Father in perfect fashion. And "whoever is not with [Him] is against [Him], and whoever does not gather with [Him] scatters."

Chapters of the Gospels

And so He says that "whoever speaks against the Holy Spirit will not be forgiven"; for the Holy Spirit does only good, and those who love good, who love God, treasure His works and eat of His fruits. But those who are evil cling to evil, and so know nothing of the goodness of God. They spit out the fruit God would give them, the goodness that cannot be denied, and take unto themselves instead the fruit of corruption. Their hearts speak nothing but malice, and such malice has no place with the good, but can only be condemned.

The Son of Man speaks truth; the Son of Man calls souls to repentance. The Son of Man will die and rise from the dead, but who will heed His wisdom, who will accept the grace of His call and become His mother and brother and sister? Only those whose hearts are set upon the Father and the doing of His will – only those whom the Spirit inspires to produce fruit unto eternity.

The Son of Man has come to heal all souls – and for what greater work could the Sabbath have been made than such healing, than such outpouring of the grace of God? Then why should any dispute with Him; why should they not thank God for the light of hope brought into their midst? He heals the mute and the blind, does He not? Is this not sign enough for anyone?

The Lord would bind Satan hand and foot and cast him from every life where he would make his home… But some will not accept the presence of Christ into their hearts, and so they but make room for the devil to return. Though the outside of their cup appear clean, yet they are empty within, void of love. And so their fruit does rot on the vine.

Humbly comes Jesus into our midst; humbly, yet with great power. Believe in Him and accept His grace, and greater than any on earth you too shall become, for you shall be one with our Savior.

> O Lord, cast all doubt and fear far from our souls;
> let our hearts be set on the kingdom of God,
> that of all good you would bring to us
> we might faithfully partake.
> Let us speak your words and live your truth.

Chapter 13 – Parables of the Kingdom

Jesus opens His mouth and speaks in parables of the kingdom of heaven. He sows the good seed of the Word of God in this chapter of parables.

Why in parables does Jesus speak? Why not in clear terms? Because the ears of those around would understand no more of the wisdom of the ages of which He speaks; and so, being told outright of the kingdom and its demands – of the end of the age and its consequences, of the final judgment and the dangers of hell – and failing to understand... what would be left for them but condemnation? Better He mask His lesson that somehow by God's grace they might later come to knowledge, or at least be kept from the full force of the wrath of God by their excuse of ignorance. (Oh why are our eyes so blind? Why can we not hear?)

But to those who do hear He explains His word that full understanding might come to them in their enlightened state and so heaven's graces pour upon their spirits. And it is indeed heaven of which our Lord speaks, and of the way we travel there.

First, make no mistake that final judgment is near, is unavoidable by any soul: we shall either be thrown into the fiery furnace or shine like the sun in the Father's kingdom. The angels will certainly separate the wicked from the righteous on the Day of the Lord. Our Lord makes this eminently clear.

Next, His parables make clear that the devil is at work in the field of the world, attempting to destroy the seed God sows and would see rise to fruitfulness. The evil one sows weeds throughout the wheat, and they grow even with God's children. He snatches the Word from the unsuspecting heart before it is even able to take root. And the flesh and the world are also at work, causing our souls to wither in sin and be choked by a vain existence.

But it is also so – and we have already stated it as a matter of course – that the Lord is indeed at work, and at work with primary force and ultimate strength. And those who are patient, those who are kind... those who would give all to find the kingdom of God will hold this fine pearl in their hands, will rise gradually to the heavens above as they maintain in their heart the Lord's overwhelming love.

Chapters of the Gospels

Listen well, my brothers and sisters. Your ears are open to hear: hear all the Lord would impart unto you. Give no dishonor to Him who is in your native place, for you are blessed to know His Word and His way. Take from your storehouse the new and the old, all that is meet to the moment, and let Him work mighty deeds among you.

> Sow your seed deep in our souls, O Lord;
> let the kingdom rise in us and with us.
> Let us bear fruit multifold
> as we glean the wisdom of your teaching.

Chapter 14 – Moved with Pity

Truly He is the Son of God, displaying great power in walking on the water, feeding the five thousand, healing all those who but touch the tassel of His cloak... and possessing a deeper compassion than any man.

Jesus' love of others is indeed on display for us here in this chapter. Upon hearing of John the Baptist's gruesome death at the hands of Herod and the whim of his illicit wife and her promiscuous daughter, the Lord but wishes to be alone to mourn for His brother and to pray to God the Father. Indeed, He withdraws "in a boat to a deserted place by Himself."

But a vast crowd follows Him, and on foot reaches the deserted place before He Himself arrives. Now, though He desires to be alone with His thoughts, His heart is "moved with pity" for the people, and He can do nothing else but cure their sicknesses.

Even as evening falls and His disciples bring a reasonable cause to send them away – there is no food in this deserted place – yet Jesus' heart goes out to the people; still He seeks their needs before His own. And so He feeds them with what little bread and fish His disciples hold.

It is not until all have had their fill and the fragments are collected (in twelve baskets, one for each apostle, with bread that comes down to us this day), that he dismisses the crowd (and His disciples) and is finally able to go alone to the mountain to pray.

Matthew

All night He spends in prayer with His Father, His heart being prepared for His sacrifice of love on the wood of the Cross. Not until the final watch of the night does He come to His disciples across the turbulent waters to calm the wind they fight. He walks quite easily upon the waves, His heart very much in another place, and even calls Peter to join Him – to teach Him the faith needed to captain the bark of His Church through the difficult times so inevitable in this life… and He reaches out His hand to save him when this yet imperfect Rock begins to sink.

Then upon reaching land, having had no sleep, He sets about healing all in the surrounding country, His mission seemingly unending and His compassion certainly unbounded.

> O Lord, your heart goes out to us.
> You are the One in whom mighty powers are at work;
> you it is who make the king of this world shake in his boots.
> But it is you, most of all, who are present to help us,
> who pity our poor souls and the death we must face.
> This fate you take upon yourself,
> and feed any need with which we come to you.
> O Lord, save us all!

Chapter 15 – Chastisement & Compassion

Difficult words and beautiful deeds from our Lord and Savior.

First, Jesus chastises the Pharisees for giving inordinate weight to the traditions of men and neglecting, and even perverting, the commands of God. These blind guides have criticized His disciples for eating with unwashed hands; but He confronts them with a harsh word regarding their taking the support that should rightly go to mother and father, and proclaims a most astounding word to all the Jews who surround Him: "It is not what enters one's mouth that defiles."

This pronouncement is not only offensive to the Pharisees but is a challenge to the very heart of Jewish culture, so set on dietary rules and regulations. Even Peter cannot understand what our Lord would here teach. But all must learn that it is the spirit and not the body that is of consequence. All must ask themselves what is in their heart.

Then Jesus gives what seems to many His harshest word, to the Canaanite woman who begs mercy for her daughter: "It is not right to take the food of the children and throw it to the dogs," thus turning aside the request of this "dog", this pagan soul. But as she persists with a faith greater than those of Israel, He cannot but answer her plea. Bowed on her knees before Him, she prevails upon the Master to do what He has not been sent to do. (Do any of us, the Lord's children of light, possess such humility as this foreigner? Should we not be shamed by her embracing of our Savior?)

Finally, toward the end of the chapter, Jesus once again reveals His great compassion for all lost souls. He readily heals "the lame, the blind, the deformed, the mute, and many others," as they are laid at His feet (much as the Cannanite made her place there as well). And when after three days with the crowd it comes time for them to depart His presence, His heart is once more moved with pity for our physical needs.

You see, though at the beginning of the chapter Jesus severely diminishes the importance of bodily matters, emphasizing as He so often does the much greater significance of the spiritual life, yet He understands our humanness, the weakness of our flesh and its requirements… and He cannot send the people off without giving them food enough to satisfy their hunger, to give them strength for the journey home.

Brothers and sisters, what a Savior have we! He cares for all with an absolute and abiding love and concern. To heal our frail souls He will offer even the harshest word.

> O Lord, you care only for saving every lost soul;
> none would you see apart from your Father's glory.
> And so, in all your words and deeds
> you draw us closer to your blessed feet,
> where we will be healed, if obediently we sit.

Chapter 16 – Divine Understanding

The sky is red with the blood of Christ. He has lain in the belly of the earth three days, and now the blood of His sacrifice covers the universe as a cleansing shower for all who take refuge in His Word and in His Cross.

Do you recognize this sign upon us even this day? Or when you look into the heavens do you see but clouds hovering overhead? Do you too think only as human beings; do you, too, fail to comprehend the Father's Word and His Son's witness? Or do you think as God, with the mind of Christ, and so see the Heaven of eternity when you look up? Do you see Jesus' face and recognize Him as the Son of the living God?

Do not be blind as the Pharisees, blind as the disciples still show themselves to be. Do not set your hearts on the bread that passes, for it is nothing, and can easily be multiplied or destroyed by the hand of the Lord. And if you gain the whole world, you will have gained nothing, for all the world will turn to dust, and you with it, when the Lord returns again.

It is the spirit that matters, the spirit about which you should be concerned, avoiding the false teaching of the proud leaders of this world and setting your heart on the word that comes from the mouth of the Lord and is spoken through His Holy Church.

In this chapter Jesus declares Peter the Rock of His Church, giving Him power to loose and bind both in heaven and on earth. Here He indeed founds His Holy Church. But this same Peter is later called "Satan" by the Lord when he seeks to save Him from the humiliation of the Cross. What is this but the clearest indication that we must have the thoughts of our heart, the very spirit within us, set upon the kingdom of God and not the concerns of the body? It is the heavenly Father who reveals to Peter that Jesus is the Messiah; but it is Peter's own flesh and blood which speaks when he calls the Lord from His sacrifice.

And, of course, the sacrifice of the Lord is the key to attaining the kingdom of God. Heaven will never be ours without the Cross. Again Jesus drives this home with His apostles, even immediately after commissioning their leader as Rock. For this is a lesson most difficult to comprehend, yet absolutely essential for all Christian souls

– if we do not lay down our lives, we will not be seated with Him on high.

The leaders of the Church must know this most of all, certainly, for theirs is the greater responsibility, the greater call... but all souls must die with Christ – must be washed clean by the blood we see in the red sky – if we are to find the glory to which all are called by the Father.

Death will have no dominion over us if we are baptized into the Lord's sacrifice.

> O Lord, how shall we join you upon the Cross?
> How shall we place all our lives into your hands?
> Let your children pray for one another,
> and your Church for all,
> that our eyes will be fixed on your heavenly kingdom
> and not on the leaven of this earth.

Chapter 17 – Transfigured Glory

Even as Jesus continues to foretell His crucifixion, that He will be given over to men and suffer and die at their hands, He reveals His transfigured glory to His three principal apostles that they might not grieve overmuch, that they might hear and understand "He will be raised on the third day."

The Lord speaks of His Transfiguration at the end of the previous chapter: "There are some standing here who will not taste death until they see the Son of Man coming in His kingdom," and six days later "Jesus [takes] Peter, James, and John his brother, and [leads] them up a high mountain," where He fulfills His prediction.

The awesome sight of the glorious Lord with Moses and Elijah is astounding enough, but it is the voice of the Father from a bright cloud which overshadows them that brings the apostles face down to the ground. But Jesus touches them and raises them up again.

Jesus would reach down and touch us all. In His great compassion He would bring the glorious majesty of almighty God to every soul. As He heals by a word the boy severely afflicted by a demon (whom even the disciples could not cure), so He would raise us all from the bondage of fear and death – if we had but faith in Him, if we but believed He is the Son of Man… if we but "listen to Him."

The Son of God has come. From God's holy mountain He has descended into our midst. Patience He has with our fears and doubts. To none would He give offense. But all must have faith, even if only the size of a mustard seed, to walk with Him who is the Temple Himself – to be joined unto His payment of our debt to those who exact blood from us.

We have nothing to give, brothers and sisters; we can do nothing without Him. But He provides for all by His sacrifice, and enables us to give payment with Him. Do not fear the greatness of God or the demands of men – Jesus lifts our poor souls to the LORD of all and protects us in all trials.

> Thank you, O Lord, for being light in our darkness.
> Though we toil blindly and in vain,
> though fear of death pervade our empty existence,
> though you yourself be taken from us…
> yet we shall believe
> and trust in your resurrection.

Chapter 18 – Forgive

We must do all we can to win our brother over to the kingdom of heaven; we must receive every child in Christ's name. We all share the responsibility of our Shepherd – His sheep must find grace in our care.

To seek to condemn we must never. To lead any soul astray we must guard against with horror. For *all* the Lord would gather in His arms – forgiveness He offers forth freely to everyone, including us, and everyone must be careful to receive well the mercy of God.

Whose debt is greater than our own, brothers and sisters? Who is less than we are? Could we ever pay back our Lord for all He has done for us; could we match His blood upon the Cross?

We have been forgiven more than we can know, and what we can know brings us to our knees. Nothing are we apart from God's love – dead would we be, tortured forever, without His grace.

Chapters of the Gospels

Yet how many of us hesitate to forgive our neighbor? How many times each day are we guilty of withholding the compassion that has been shown our souls? Let us not be so blind, brothers and sisters. Let us remember always the Lord's favor to us, and share it so freely with others.

To the torturers let us not come; the millstone around our necks let us avoid at all cost. Neither hand nor foot nor eye means anything if we grieve the Lord, for then we will lose the kingdom of God.

Should we exalt ourselves? Should we even ask the Lord who is first in heaven? No thought of this kind should enter our hearts; rather, we should seek to be as humble as by God we may be.

How many times should we forgive our brother? – how many times has the Lord forgiven us? Do you not know? Can you not see? Though all must be done to save our brother from the fault that might plague his days, yet our sole concern should be to bring him to repentance; our sole desire should be that we might forgive him. For, as it is for Jesus our Shepherd, so we must wish that even the most lost individual comes to the forgiveness of God.

Let all temptation to sin and to judge be cast into the sea. Let us free our brothers from any torture which awaits them. Then we will be in league with our Savior, who is certainly first in the kingdom of heaven.

> O Lord, like a little child let us be.
> Set us in your midst,
> graced with your forgiveness and humility.
> Give us the same heart as you hold,
> that upon the salvation of all souls ours might be set.
> Thank you for your mercy, Lord.

Chapter 19 – For the Kingdom

The bond of marriage and the call to religious life. Both shock the disciples, who wonder how a man can be expected to remain ever faithful to his wife, and also how a rich man will enter the kingdom of God. In both cases all things must be given up – both our hardness of heart and the possessions to which we are attached.

Matthew

Our Lord certainly seems to favor the life of a religious, who renounces marriage and all earthly goods. "Whoever can accept this ought to accept it," He says of remaining celibate for the kingdom of heaven. And He would have the soul who entreats Him be "perfect" by selling all he owns and following Him strictly on the way to salvation. But He also cautions that this call is not for all, but only those to whom it is granted.

And lest we think there is something demeaning about the call to marriage, in the short account which serves as a hinge to our two primary scenes (the Pharisees' questioning about the indissolubility of marriage and the rich man's questioning about eternal life), our Lord makes clear the blessing of children – the fruit of marriage – by stating, "The kingdom of heaven belongs to such as these."

Whether we are children in fact or children in spirit (who give up everything to follow Christ) or those who are bonded together to bring children into the world, the Lord's call is upon us all. Yes, those who give up "houses or brothers or sisters or father or mother or children or lands for the sake of [Christ's] Name" will be greatly blessed in His heavenly reign; but this does not mean that those who accomplish the difficult goal of remaining wed to one spouse their whole lives through will not be blessed by the Lord. They will be blessed with children, and these children will be a blessing for the kingdom, if they are given to God as His own... if they are brought to Jesus to lay His hands upon.

Keep the commandments well, my brothers and sisters, and teach others to do the same. And if you feel called to be perfect even as our Savior is perfect (as the heavenly Father is perfect), then do not be afraid for what you will lose in this cause. Rather, raise your eyes to see Him who calls you in love, and know that there is great blessing in this Word upon your soul.

But if to this you are not called, do not attempt to follow thus anyway – for it will be in vain. And though you think you are first in His kingdom, you will find yourself last of all.

> All things let us give to you, O Lord,
> whether we hold them in our arms or in our hearts.
> Take from us whatever you will,
> for our souls seek but the glory of the new world.
> Let your age dawn upon our eyes

that we might rise to your light
in faith and in trust in you.

Chapter 20 – Laborers in the Vineyard

Here the Lord seeks to open our eyes (as He does those of the blind men at the chapter's end) to the empty call of this world to "lord it over" others, and to the blessings upon those who lay down their lives for the kingdom.

The parable of the workers in the vineyard follows immediately upon Jesus' words regarding the difficulty the rich have entering the kingdom of heaven, presented in the chapter before. Now the lesson is of the work we are called by the owner of the vineyard to accomplish as laborers in His fields.

Those who work long, who bear "the day's burden and the heat," come with expectations of greater reward than promised them when they see the others who have worked so much less receiving the same amount. And they are angry not to be given what seems to them an appropriate bonus.

Jesus is teaching us first, as He has elsewhere and often, that we are unworthy servants who but do the work provided by God. We deserve nothing in return for our labor. Yet He is trying to convey more than this to His disciples. He would have us understand also what a blessing it is to bear the heat of the day with Him, to suffer with Him. This grace we can only realize if our eyes and hearts are not set on the rewards of earth – as are the apostles' in seeking special consideration – but on His heavenly kingdom.

This is confirmed in Jesus' statement and question to James and John: "You do not know what you are asking. Can you drink the cup that I am going to drink?" For they would sit at His right and left hand in the kingdom, they would be most exalted, but this requires suffering under the Cross He bears, and that without complaint, and that with joy.

We are called by Jesus to serve and not to be served, to give our lives as a ransom for the many, bearing whatever burden the Lord places upon us. As the landowner generously gives full pay even to those who work but an hour, as Christ Himself reaches out to touch and heal the eyes of the two blind men begging by the side of the road – as ever He would take the least among us and raise them up to the dignity only He possesses, so must we all do, with a heart of absolute concern and service for our fellow man. We must drink this cup of which our Savior drinks if we hope to sit with Him.

Follow Him up the road of sacrifice, brothers and sisters. Follow Him to Jerusalem, where the tree awaits.

> O Lord, let us not be concerned for our pay
> or for the prestige we might hope to find.
> Let our hearts be set on pouring out our blood
> in the heat of the day,
> upon your Cross.
> Your labor let us complete.

Chapter 21 – Zeal for God's House

In actions and in parables, and in direct statement, Jesus reveals that He is the Son of David purifying the temple of God for the coming kingdom.

Jesus enters Jerusalem "meek and riding on an ass," but powerfully it is made known that He is the Son of God. The road before Him is strewn with cloaks and cut branches as the people cry "Hosanna in the highest" to our Lord and Savior. The whole city is "shaken" as the great Prophet enters.

And once in the temple area the cries do not cease but increase, coming even from the mouths of children. Jesus overturns "the tables of the money changers," driving out those engaged "in selling and buying," in a great display of zeal for God's "house of prayer." The blind and the lame are cured as the thieves in charge of the temple become indignant.

These scribes and Pharisees, these leaders of the people, will be cast from their place, and the kingdom of God will be given over to those of faith who merit its grace. Though these false teachers kill the Lord and throw Him out of the vineyard, this cornerstone of the Temple, this only Son of the living God, shall crush them, and they will wither in a moment, even as the fig tree He curses.

Chapters of the Gospels

And those who seemed to be outcasts, the tax collectors and prostitutes who have turned to the Lord at the preaching of John – indeed all the Gentile nations who genuinely seek the face of God – shall enter into the Temple, find their place in the kingdom of heaven… even as the unfaithful son is destroyed.

It is John the Baptist who has prepared the way of the Lord, more than the branches before Him on the path to Jerusalem. John's baptism was of heavenly origin, and those who believed him are blessed, those who accepted his word now know the Savior – but those who did not know John do not know Jesus either, and so will find no place in the kingdom.

Do not question Jesus' authority. Do not put Him to the test or selfishly seek a salvation of your own making, greedily attempting to depose the Son of the living God from His rightful place. Though He bleed at your hands, your murderous actions will be in vain.

Rather, turn to Him and cry out as children in innocence and in faith of the great glory that has entered your midst, and lay all that you own at His feet.

> Hosanna to the King of kings!
> The Lord of lords! The Son of David
> and Son of God!
> Let us drink of the fruit of your vineyard, Lord,
> in the New Jerusalem.
> Alleluia!

Chapter 22 – No Questions

No more questions will any dare to ask Him anymore. The Pharisees and their disciples, the Sadducees and scholars of the law – those who refuse His invitation to the wedding feast – step forward to trap Him in His words… but Jesus silences them all.

And all are left "amazed" and "astonished" at the teaching that issues forth from His mouth, at His absolute power and authority. None can trip Him up for none has wisdom greater than He who is the love of the Father Himself and who loves like no other.

Matthew

"Give to Caesar what belongs to Caesar"; "He is not the God of the dead but the living"; "If David calls Him 'Lord', how can He be his son?" Every question is answered to the point, with undeniable proof, with divine wisdom. And so none can be left in any doubt that this is the Son of God and that all should listen to Him, and come when He calls.

Let us obtain our wedding garment, brothers and sisters. Though all are gathered into the kingdom's hall, not all are suited to remain – and to be then cast out would be the most dreadful thing. We must prepare ourselves well, obedient to God's word. Though we give to the world what is owed to it in taxes and otherwise, our very souls must be given to God, for His alone are we now and ever.

If we do not worship the Lord, if we do not pay Him due honor, how can we expect to be prepared to enter His presence, where nothing but praise will come from our mouths?

And the resurrection we will not know, or at least know well, if our faith is not strong. If we doubt the power of God and are blind to the Scriptures, lost will we, too, ever be… apart from the Lord above.

Love God. This is your call; this is His command. Do we doubt those whom we love? Do we question their motives and intentions? Do we say they do not exist? Love God and love neighbor – this is the foundation of our faith. None is beyond the pale for our Lord to save and so none should we write off as dead. But all must be encouraged to love.

"What is your opinion about the Messiah?" Is He subject to any man? Is there one greater than He? Or is He indeed the Son of God, and God Himself? Then why do you not believe in Him?

> Let us be silent before your awesome power, O Lord;
> let us but listen to the word you speak.
> For nothing but truth flows from your lips,
> and to nothing but glory do you lead us all.
> May your love be our garment for the kingdom.

Chapters of the Gospels

Chapter 23 – Chastising Love

O the woe of the scribes and the Pharisees! O the power of the chastising Word of Christ! O the love found in such utter truth.

At the end of the previous chapter Jesus had silenced all questions, particularly regarding His authority, showing to the Pharisees how the Son of David is also Lord over David. And now the Messiah lets loose with perhaps His most powerful and penetrating discourse, which is, I'm sure, most difficult for Him to speak, but which must be exclaimed for the sake of all straying souls… and which will lead to His crucifixion.

Here in His final public teaching in the Gospel of Matthew – He will speak to His disciples privately in the subsequent two chapters, but will not speak to the crowds or the Pharisees again (thus fulfilling what He declares at the end of the chapter: "I tell you, you will not see me again until you say, 'Blessed is He who comes in the Name of the Lord.'") – Jesus excoriates the scribes and Pharisees, bringing up before their eyes and the eyes of the crowds (for it is before all that He details their sins) one after the other of the woes these proud souls invite upon themselves, woes that lead directly to Gehenna.

But these words are meant not only for the Pharisees, of course, but for all ears, all of Jerusalem – which He makes quite clear in His final lament, His final cry over the city of God. All His children He would gather beneath His wings, but all are unwilling! If the leaders of the people are held up for their evil, it is only meet to their responsibility. But who is not guilty of killing the prophets, of crucifying the Son of God?

Two other important points must be kept in mind, for they are too often overlooked. The first is that Jesus prefaces His railing against Israel's leaders by stating, "The scribes and the Pharisees have taken their seat on the chair of Moses. Therefore, do and observe all things they tell you." Though He warns against following their example, though He declares openly and repeatedly that they are "hypocrites," yet He gives no one permission to deny their authority – for their authority comes from God, and to deny it is to deny God Himself. Despite their sins, their teaching *must* be respected. (This same power rests now upon Peter and the apostles, upon the Pope and the bishops of the Church – and it too must always be heeded.)

The other point of importance to be kept firmly in mind is that "whom the Lord loves, He disciplines; He scourges every son He acknowledges." As St. Paul asks, "What 'son' is there whom his father does not discipline?" and pointedly states, "If you are without discipline, you are not sons but bastards" (Heb.12:7,8). So do not think the Lord lacks of love for the scribes and Pharisees (or for ourselves for that matter). He loves them all the more if His chastisement is all the greater. His heart bleeds deeply for their souls. He would not see them continue as "blind guides" and "whitewashed tombs," and so when He calls them "serpents" and a "brood of vipers," you must hear that His heart cries out for their salvation, in great lament for the path they have chosen. Our own eyes should fill with tears at the woes coming upon them, tears for the great truth (and justice) being revealed by the Messiah, tears for the love of all our Savior embodies (a love that leads to the Cross) – tears for all the sins that draw the blood of the righteous and tears calling for our salvation.

> O Lord, could you spend yourself any more
> for our salvation?
> Could your love come from a deeper source?
> Your cry of truth that chastises our souls
> overwhelms us with your encompassing love.
> Thank you, O Lord, for we know it is hard
> to see your children so far astray –
> and harder still to scourge the sons
> whom you simply love so much.
> Let all be redeemed by your Cross.

Chapter 24 – The Tribulation

As Jesus is leaving the temple area after His final public discourse, the disciples point out to Him the beauty of the temple's structure – but He only speaks of its imminent destruction, and then the imminent destruction of all the world.

Seated on the Mount of Olives, the place His Passion will begin, the Lord speaks privately to His disciples of His second coming and the end of the age. Though no one (not even the Son) knows when this will be, our Savior relates the signs of these times and how we should be on our guard.

First, there will be many false prophets pretending to be the Messiah, who would, if possible, deceive even the elect of God. The vanity of their signs and wonders will be perceived only by the elect, who will be preserved, by God's grace, from the clutches of the evil come upon the world. And so, we must not chase after the false idols of the age, or into condemnation we will come, and so wail and grind our teeth with the profligate of this degenerate place.

There will be great tribulation on the Day of the Lord, yes. We will have to endure sorrows and suffering, trials and persecution, for wars will come with famine and earthquake, and the very foundation of the earth will be shaken along with the powers of heaven, as sun and moon darken and the stars fall from the sky.

But when the time has come, the Lord will make Himself known. From one end of the sky to the other His light will shine, and none will be able to deny His power. He will be at the gate then, ready to enter, to break in upon a fallen world… but till He comes, be patient, and endure what must come first.

Certainly we must watch over ourselves, and watch closely. We cannot "eat and drink with drunkards," giving ourselves to the sins of the flesh as those in the time of Noah and becoming thereby hardened to the Word of the Lord. No, to faithfulness and prudence the Messiah calls us, to serving Him and doing His will day in and day out upon this plane.

If we remain faithful to God, the tribulation will soon pass us by, for the Lord will shorten it for our sake. So do not fear the darkening of the sun or the temple walls being thrown down – if the earth should quake it is but to awaken it to truth. Thus, if we seek truth and remain set in love, we should only welcome the coming of the Christ at the end of time. And once the abominations of this world are duly destroyed, He will welcome His elect with open arms; they will be gathered in by the angels.

> O Lord, let your Word go forth to the ends of the earth,
> that all men might be prepared for your coming.
> Stay close to us, dear Jesus, and teach us well –
> look with mercy on your disciples.
> Though we share your passion and must bleed for you,

yet our faith will keep us as we fly to your heaven.
A corpse let us not remain.

Chapter 25 – The Final Judgment

Jesus concludes His discourse with His disciples on His coming at the end of the age with two parables and one real account of the final judgment. They make clear that in the end the wicked "will go off to eternal punishment, but the righteous to eternal life." And they serve as perhaps the best chapter of refutation against those who minimize, if not eliminate, man's own responsibility for his salvation, revealing undeniably what James has so succinctly stated: "Faith without works is dead" (2:26).

The parable of the ten virgins points up the special need for us to be wise about our preparation for our Savior's coming. We must not only "stay awake" since we know "neither the day nor the hour" of the Bridegroom's return, but we must also have sufficient oil for our lamps. The lamps alone, a kind of superficial light, will not do – there must be depth to our teaching and understanding. We must be as seed planted firmly in good earth, in the teaching and sacraments of the Church, if we expect to keep our light shining long after the time of worldly matters has passed. Or the coming darkness will overtake us and we will not be able to stand, not be able to grow… All our hearts must be set on readiness for the kingdom.

In the parable of the ten talents the Lord makes obvious our need to *work* with the gifts He gives us. He provides the grace, He provides our talents, but if we are not industrious with what is provided, we shall lose it in the end. Whereas if we toil well here in our Savior's absence, our faithful service will receive a rich reward. Whatever the Lord gives us must be put to use if we are to come into the kingdom of God.

Finally, Jesus states explicitly upon what criteria He will judge the nations, and every soul upon this plane. We are only "blessed by [His] Father," we will only "inherit the kingdom prepared for [us] from the foundation of the world," if we do as He has commanded and serve Him in the least of our brothers. If we do not lay down our lives, if we do not feed the hungry, give drink to the thirsty, welcome the stranger, clothe the naked, care for the ill, and visit those in prison – in short, if we do not bring His light into the darkness of this world and raise souls from the pit into which they fall… we shall not know Him nor He us, and a word of condemnation alone will be ours.

The eternal fire let us avoid, brothers and sisters, by employing well our love in wisdom and in patience with all our strength all the days before our Master's return, and that return will be a day of joy – and on that day we will enter the kingdom of heaven.

> O Lord, prepare us well for your coming.
> Keep us on right paths with you
> with hearts of service
> and the wisdom only you hold,
> that when you come
> we shall rejoice
> and feast at your table.

Chapter 26 – The Passion Begins

The Passion begins. The Son of Man is handed over on the feast of Passover.

Here indeed the sufferings begin, and begin to accumulate: the chief priests and elders conspire to arrest the Lord; His three principal apostles fall asleep three times on His desperate request for prayer (and so the cup will not pass from Him); the crowds come against Him with swords and clubs, as if against a robber, led by Judas His betrayer; He is brought before false witnesses and must endure their lying testimony, and then their spit in His face and hands across His cheeks. Finally, Peter, His Rock, denies Him three times.

Quite alone is Jesus left in His Passion, to fulfill the Scripture of the Suffering Servant condemned for our sins. But all He receives with patience and resolve, remaining silent when He could call down "twelve legions of angels."

Yes, quite freely does He give Himself to us, accepting the anointing of His body for burial, stepping forward when they come to arrest Him… facing death and the torture of unfaithful souls with absolute trust in the Father.

Matthew

And here in His Passion, at its very inception, He offers the Sacrament of salvation that will remain with us till the end of the age, till all His suffering is filled up in the Body of Christ... to impart His eternal presence to us in this substantial way.

"This is my body." "This is my blood of the covenant." The body that will soon be raised on the Cross, the blood that will soon be poured forth for man's sins, is here wholly offered to His disciples, to all who sit with Him at table. Before He ever goes to the Mount of Olives, before He ever enters the garden of Gethsemane, here He dies already for each of us. He does not hesitate to pour Himself out.

Agony comes. Agony and betrayal. The end is upon Him as the sins of man mount up before His eyes. None stand at His side. But His sole concern, even as He is delivered into the hands of the prince of darkness, is the forgiveness of those who are the devil's blind instruments. His only desire is to shed His blood that we might be cleansed.

> Our cry goes up before you, Lord:
> with Peter we weep bitterly for our sins.
> May we not fall asleep on you now;
> may we never deny your divinity.
> Though we have all done evil in your sight,
> let your sacrifice redeem our lives,
> your love encompass our disobedience.
> Our flesh make strong in your body and blood.

Chapter 27 – The Way of the Cross

The deed is done. The Son of God is crucified. Here is the way of the Cross.

Indeed, this chapter begins with the condemnation of Jesus and ends with His burial, thus addressing the same frame of events reflected in our popular devotion, the Stations of the Cross. Here the Lord endures the accusations in silence, bears the cry of the crowd for His crucifixion, and listens to the sentence passed by Pilate as he washes his hands. Here He is scourged, plaited with a crown of thorns, and roundly mocked by the whole cohort of soldiers. Here He is driven to the Place of the Skull (Simon of Cyrene at His side only to hasten His journey), stripped of His clothes, nailed to the Cross, and subjected to the reviling tongues of the crowds, the chief priests, scribes and elders, and even the criminals either side of Him... all as He dies on the Cross for our sins.

Finally, He cries out to God; finally, He raises His voice in the darkness... and then dies, giving His Spirit into His Father's hands. Then the earth quakes. Then the veil of the temple is torn in two and the tombs are broken open, the dead saints coming forth and walking the earth. Then even the soldiers' knees shake, and they cannot but say: "Truly, this was the Son of God!"

He is taken down from the Cross. He is laid in a tomb. And the tomb is sealed and guarded.

All this to the King of the Jews. All this to the Savior of the human race. Such suffering is His alone. Only He could endure it all in silence.

And perhaps the turning point comes – the decision made, the sentence passed, His death pronounced – upon the words the "whole people" declare to Pilate: "His blood be upon us and upon our children." The guilt they take upon themselves they know not, but it is enough to ensure the Messiah's crucifixion.

This must come; yes, all of this must transpire. The Son of God must suffer greatly for our sins before being raised again on the third day. And it must be His children who take His blood upon themselves. Who else but the Jews, the Chosen of God, could call His blood down on themselves? But it is indeed so, that all souls are responsible for the death of Christ. And until any soul knows his bloodguilt, he shall not come to the salvation known only in the cleansing by that same blood.

> O Lord, your blood is upon us all;
> your suffering you endured because of all our sins.
> Let your blood be upon us now to bring us to redemption.
> For all you have borne for us
> we praise you, Lord –
> and we wait by your tomb.
> May we be forgiven our sins against your flesh...
> O Son of God, O King on High,
> rise from the dead!

Chapter 28 – The Empty Tomb

A rather brief account of the Lord's resurrection, comprised of the angel's rolling back of the stone from the tomb, his telling the women to inform the disciples of Jesus' rising (and the Lord's own appearing to them along the way), the chief priests' bribing the guards to say His body was stolen away, and Jesus' commissioning of His disciples.

The rolling back of the stone is said to have caused "a great earthquake" and the angel's appearance said to have been "like lightning" – truly dramatic is this moment of Truth, this moment our eyes witness that our Savior is no longer in the tomb, that He has been raised.

And the divergent paths of truth and lie are quite evident: as the women go their way bearing the Good News, the guards go to the priests, who concoct their enduring tale.

Finally, the words of the Lord to His disciples are to the point – make disciples, baptize them, teach them… His power is with us until the end of the age.

> O Lord, you have risen
> and history is changed.
> Now does light come to this world
> in the fullness of truth.
> May we be disciples obedient to your word,
> and so offer you due homage.

Chapters of the Gospels

II.

The Gospel of Mark

Chapters of the Gospels

Chapter 1 – The Mission Begins

His way is prepared, He calls His disciples, and He begins His preaching and healing mission.

Two (or three) quotes stand out in this initial chapter of Mark. First, though the Lord's way is prepared greatly by the preaching of John the Baptist – by his appearance in the desert and his proclamation of a baptism of repentance for the forgiveness of sins, that Jesus might meet souls ready for His coming – Jesus Himself is prepared for the mission He is about to undertake by the temptations He suffers in the desert. Of these forty days it is written, "He was among wild beasts, and the angels ministered to Him." Once having entered upon His path of preaching and healing in this lost world, what beasts will surround our Savior, what demons will conspire to knock down His door – and so, how He will need the angels' protection. And so He is made ready for what will come.

And how attractive is the Truth among us. How souls are drawn to the Messiah, the Holy One of God! The disciples leave their nets immediately to follow Him; the crowds, astonished at the authority of His teaching and amazed at His power over unclean spirits, come from all over to hear Him and be healed by His touch. When He enters the house of Simon Peter's mother-in-law (whom He raises up from a fever), we are told, "The whole town was gathered at the door," and later that – despite His repeated attempts to silence the demons who knew who He was, His seeking the solitude of deserted places, and His insistence that those whom He heals "tell no one" – His fame continued to spread, and indeed, "people kept coming to Him from everywhere."

Who can control the desire for truth? Who can temper the longing for healing? Who is not like the leper seeking pity, reaching out to be made clean? Though souls might harden themselves against these innate needs, yet when the One who can supply our deepest desires stands before us, who can resist?

Prepare the way of the Lord, brothers and sisters. He will baptize you with the Holy Spirit if you come to His presence among us now, if you heed His call to faith and salvation.

> The time is fulfilled, we know, O Lord;
> your hand is stretched forth to cure our ills.
> Your Word now goes out to the ends of the earth...
> May we kneel down and knock upon your door,
> that to us the kingdom may be opened.

Chapter 2 – New Wine

Mark continues to speak of the "many who followed Him" – illustrating the crush of the people upon the Savior most poignantly in the paralytic's being lowered to Jesus through the roof of a crowded house – but the consistent theme of this chapter is that "new wine is poured into fresh wineskins."

Question upon question comes to the Lord as He repeatedly seems to break the old law: "Who but God alone can forgive sins?" "Why does He eat with tax collectors and sinners?" "Why do...[His] disciples...not fast?" "Why are they doing what is unlawful on the Sabbath?"

But, of course, Jesus always has answer: He can forgive sins because He has the authority of God. Far from being contaminated by eating with sinners, He serves as their physician, making them clean. Who can fast in the glory of God's presence? And, "The Sabbath was made for man, not man for the Sabbath." In short: "The Son of Man is Lord even of the Sabbath." He is the Son of God, God Himself, and the Law He brings supersedes and fulfills that of old... for it is wholly of love. And no genuine concern for the welfare of others can ever be against God's will.

I think this message can be discovered in the few words Mark uses to describe the Lord's apprehension of the four men struggling to get their friend into His midst. He says of our Savior's reaction to the men's lowering the mat with the paralytic through the opened roof: "Jesus saw their faith." It is faith Jesus is looking for, faith He has come to find. For witnessing it in us (and notice that faith is *seen* in actions), He can save our souls and so accomplish His mission – but without it we go away empty.

Mercy and love are what the Lord brings, and no law is broken by these. For God is all-merciful, God is all-loving, and we must have

Chapters of the Gospels

fresh wineskins to receive Him. No doubt or question of His mighty and merciful presence can remain in us, or we will be hardened from coming to Him.

> O Lord, your grace upon our souls we seek;
> your Word we treasure with all our hearts.
> Let us be wed unto you and your way,
> that we might glorify God at work in our lives.

Chapter 3 – The Crush of the Crowd

This chapter begins as the previous one ended, with Jesus challenging the Pharisees about the law, particularly regarding the Sabbath. Before their accusatory gaze He brings a man with a withered hand. In the midst of the people in the synagogue on the Sabbath He asks them what could be a most enlightening question: "Is it lawful to do good on the Sabbath?" The answer is obvious and His healing the man is certainly a good act – but their hearts are hardened against Him, and now they can only seek to put Him to death.

The key line of the chapter (and perhaps of Mark's whole Gospel), though, is – "Those who had diseases were pressing upon Him to touch Him." In a most descriptive phrase, we are told Jesus asked for a boat that the crowd "would not crush Him." (O what a Savior! who will be crushed for our sins, who will be ground like wheat and trampled like grapes, that we might eat of His body and drink of His blood.)

It is this overwhelming outpouring of desire for the Lord's presence that indeed characterizes this chapter. People again coming in large numbers from everywhere necessitates Jesus' appointing of the twelve apostles, that they too might go out and preach and heal. It is when the crowds gather so that He and His apostles cannot even eat, that His family begins to fear for His life and say, "He is out of His mind." And, of course, it is out of jealousy for the intensity of the fervor all souls have for their Savior that the scribes from Jerusalem state, "He is possessed by Beelzebul," and begin to plot His crucifixion.

Finally, it is interesting to note that in the same chapter that Jesus names His apostles, He also makes the declaration, "Whoever does the will of God is my brother and sister and mother." All are gathered into His home and into His arms; none does He reject. All become as sons of the heavenly Father, as He is, because of His zealous love for man. How happy we should be that our Lord has come among us, set us free from the power of Satan, and made us as His own brothers and sisters and mother. Turn not from such grace, but embrace your God.

> O Lord, you call us all –
> you heal us all and make us your own.
> What joy there is at your coming!
> What hope we have now of salvation!
> Let your Word go forth to the ends of the earth;
> let it drive out demons every hour of every day...
> Break the hold of Satan
> and let your Spirit rush upon us.
> Alleluia!

Chapter 4 – Hear and Believe

We must bear fruit thirty, sixty, and a hundredfold. We must place our lamps upon a stand and let our light shine forth for all to see, ever growing greater in the gifts and graces of the Lord. But first we must have faith. Faith alone makes our soil rich and provides oil for our lamp. Faith is the mustard seed that sprouts and grows to eternal life.

Jesus teaches through the course of a day seated in a boat by the shoreline. The crowds and His disciples gather round to listen. To the people He speaks in parables, but to those closest to Him, He explains His teaching.

His teaching is of the kingdom of God. His teaching is of the Word that goes forth, that is sown in this world for all to hear, that all might come to the kingdom. "Whoever has ears to hear ought to hear," Jesus proclaims, a declaration recorded twice in this chapter. It is the Lord's will that we should listen, that we should hear, that we should heed His word and grow in His light. But how many have

Chapters of the Gospels

hearts that are set on the kingdom – how many have the faith necessary to hear?

Too many are distracted. Too many fall away at the bruising of a reed, at the least trial. Far too many are concerned with the riches of this world. And so Satan swallows too many; and so a great many wither away or are choked by the thorns of temptation. And so, many do not bear fruit… and so, many do not enter the kingdom.

At the end of the chapter the disciples of the Christ are tested. It is the end of the day. They have listened to the Lord's teaching and had its meaning laid out for them. And now, still in the boat, they cross the sea. A violent storm comes up, waves breaking over the sides… and Jesus is asleep. And they are terrified. They do not pass their test of faith.

The Lord rises and rebukes and stills the wind and the waves, then asks His disciples: "Do you not yet have faith?" Though their ears have been filled with His words, their seed ground is not yet prepared to bear fruit.

And what of us, brothers and sisters? Do we yet wonder who He is? Or do we believe? (Do we hear?)

> O Lord, open my heart to receive your Word
> and let it grow unto heaven.
> Never let me be apart from your light,
> fearful of the storms of this world.
> Though I know not how it does occur,
> let me rise each day toward your kingdom.

<u>Chapter 5</u> – Powerful Cures

Three particularly remarkable cures: the Gerasene demoniac, the woman with the hemorrhages, and Jairus' daughter. The power of the Lord knows no bounds.

The demoniac comes from the tombs where he dwells to prostrate himself before Jesus. Here is a man whom shackles and chains could not bind, who "night and day among the tombs and on the hillsides… was always crying out and bruising himself with stones." But here is a man, and a legion of devils, reduced to dust before the Son of the

Mark

Most High God. And by a word from Jesus' mouth, the man is soon found "clothed and in his right mind," seated at the feet of his Savior.

The woman afflicted with hemorrhages for twelve years, who had spent all she had to find a cure but only grew worse, who "had suffered at the hands of many doctors," now comes through the dense crowd to touch the Physician of all men's bodies and souls… and in an instant she is healed.

And the official's daughter, a child of twelve, is declared dead. People are found weeping and wailing loudly outside her house. But the Lord goes inside. He touches her hand. He tells her to arise, and she hears His penetrating voice – a voice, a Word, a Spirit that conquers even death – and at once she is obedient, walking around in the room that a moment before had seemed her tomb.

To what extent will the Lord not go? Where is it His power cannot reach? Who is there that cannot be healed? Who is beyond His love, His sacrifice for our sins?

None, we know. None is outside His grasp, beyond the saving power of His touch and His word. He is Lord of all, and the very tombs we erect He smashes to dust – death itself is at His command.

> All the earth is in your hand, dear God.
> Your Son has power over every created thing.
> And all who come to Him shall be cured;
> the light He brings is salvation for every soul.
> So let us draw near your presence, wherever we are.
> Let us call upon you to draw near to us…
> that no death or torment shall remain,
> that *we* shall be found in right body and mind
> in your eternal kingdom.

Chapter 6 – Hardened Hearts

Great numbers of people continue to press upon Jesus, but not in His native place. Those "among His own kin" turn away from the Messiah in doubt of Him whom they know only as a man. And so these do not receive His grace; His mighty deeds cannot break in upon their lack of faith.

Chapters of the Gospels

But to all the word of God must go forth, whether accepted or rejected. Thus the Lord sends out the Twelve to the surrounding towns to preach repentance and heal the sick. They go empty of hand but filled with the Spirit of God, and some welcome them while others stand against them.

In the midst of this chapter is a kind of digression addressing Herod's reaction to Jesus' fame and recounting the story of the Baptist's beheading. Herod's fear of John is greatly in evidence here, in his inability to keep from listening to the prophet's chastisements and his distress at being unable to prevent his execution, yes, but especially in his thought that John has returned to haunt him in the person of Jesus. (Do you see how each soul is confronted with the truth of God?)

When the apostles return from their mission, they have "no opportunity even to eat" for the people that press upon them, and so Jesus would take them to a deserted place. But that deserted place is quickly filled with needy souls, and so there is no rest for the weary, as there is no pause in Jesus' pity.

When the apostles point out that "this is a deserted place and it is already very late," suggesting the people be dismissed to find something to eat, one can almost hear their own stomachs grumble as evening draws on. We then hear the Lord offer one of His most challenging lines: "Give them some food yourselves." It is a remarkably unreasonable request made of exhausted and starving men, but they must be taught to trust in the Lord, and not to fear the laying down of their lives.

After the miracle of the feeding of the five thousand (with five loaves and two fish) has taken place, we learn something revealing, and disturbing, about the apostles of the Lord at this time.

They are tossed about on the waves of the sea through the night, and when Jesus approaches, walking on the water, they are utterly terrified at what they perceive to be a ghost. Once the Lord enters and so calms their boat, Mark tells us of their lack of faith, for yet their eyes are blind to who He is; even the miracle of the loaves they failed to understand because "their hearts were hardened," even as their stomachs were finally fed.

But Jesus continues to teach and to heal, and they continue to accompany Him. All bring their sick on mats to Him, in great faith of His merest touch. Yet His apostles – who even heal these themselves

Mark

– still share in part the ignorance of Herod and Jesus' townspeople toward the Son of Man.

> O Lord, leave us not in blindness;
> take from our souls any vain fear.
> Open our hearts to see your wonders
> and who it is has visited us,
> that we might feed upon your flesh
> and welcome you into our home.

Chapter 7 – Seeking Refuge

That Jesus would find a certain refuge from the souls that continually press upon Him becomes evident in this chapter, wherein the Lord seeks still to enlighten His people regarding the ways of God.

The questions now come to Jesus about the cleansing of hands (and "cups and jugs and kettles..."): Why is it His disciples eat with hands unwashed? How can they break "the tradition of the elders"? And so the Lord is given occasion to reproach them for the vanity of their worship, which focuses so on the passing body while ignoring correction of the interior works of the soul, from which all evil comes.

Here He declares all foods clean, and even His disciples are "without understanding." How slowly we come to the things of the Spirit. How dull are our hearts to the teaching of God.

And, perhaps overwhelmed by the blindness of all people as well as by their press upon Him, Jesus "went off to the district of Tyre. He entered a house and wanted no one to know about it." In this foreign land, in this unknown house, He looks to find a measure of quiet and peace, "but He could not escape notice." And soon a foreign woman, a Greek, not of the house of Israel, breaks in upon His sanctuary to beg the healing of her daughter. And even she is able to move the Lord to pity. (How can His heart not be moved?)

Then when about to heal a deaf man back in His own land, "He took him off by himself away from the crowd." How can He heal in the din that surrounds Him? How can He perform works of faith in the midst of many whose worship is vain? And so, alone He must be

Chapters of the Gospels

with His patient and God. It is to heaven He ever looks, away from the sickness of this land.

Of His healing, "He ordered them not to tell anyone. But the more He ordered them not to, the more they proclaimed it." The Father's will must be done, despite the agony it brings to His soul, for the Son is obedient to the Father – the cup shall not pass from Him.

> O Lord, open our ears,
> we who remain deaf to your silence,
> to your presence even in this empty world.
> Open our hearts to your cleansing Word,
> that we might honor you not only with our lips
> but with our very lives.
> In understanding of your Spirit let us now dwell
> as your faithful children.

<u>Chapter 8</u> – Gradual Understanding

Perhaps the central point of this chapter is that it is only gradually that Christ's disciples come to genuine understanding of the presence of the Messiah. This is exemplified in His healing of the blind man of Bethsaida – for the first time Jesus touches him, the man sees people "looking like trees and walking," whereas after the second touch he "sees everything distinctly" – and is evident in His apostles' still "not thinking as God does, but as human beings do," both in their failure to recognize His power in the breaking of the bread for the multitude (repeated in this chapter) and in their desire to keep Him from the sacrifice that leads to eternal life for all. Still their eyes look more to the bread of earth than that of heaven.

Of this preoccupation with earthly matters, which the Lord terms "the leaven of the Pharisees" – particularly regarding their seeking a sign, an amazing miracle at their own command – He would cure them. Such blindness to His love, to His divine presence among them (even after all His miraculous cures and astounding teaching), causes Jesus to sigh "from the depth of His spirit." His desire that souls seek not the show of signs but the light of God in their lives is illustrated in His instructions to the blind man after his healing: "Do not even go into the village." Rather, He sends him home to go about his life and work in faith and in quiet, knowing the Lord is with him.

As for the apostles, though Peter declares Jesus the Messiah and certainly all the others agree, yet they do not really know Him; still the Cross He carries is hidden from their eyes and from their hearts. So He rebukes Peter for trying to prevent His journey to Jerusalem and His death, calling him a "Satan". So He summons the crowd and proclaims the necessity of the Cross in the life of any of His disciples.

Not until we see the Cross as central to His call and accept it upon our own shoulders will we begin to know truly who Jesus is; not until then will we understand His words, our eyes open to the Spirit speaking in Him. (It is only after three days in the wilderness with Jesus that the people are fed by His hand; those who do not share His Passion do not know the Lord or eat at His table.)

One final note on the chapter: here is clearly illustrated the fact that Peter speaks for all the apostles, that he is first among them, and so Pope. Certainly this is revealed in his declaration to Jesus, "You are the Messiah," for all believe, though only one speaks. But more particularly it is discernible in the manner in which the Lord rebukes the Rock of His Church. He calls Peter "Satan" while "looking at His disciples" to convey that what they all now think but only Peter speaks – i.e. that His death must be avoided – is not in accord with the will of God... and so to chastise them all through the one.

A sense of this 'misdirection', of this emphasis to one by speaking to others, is present also in Jesus' telling the crowd of the call of the Cross that His apostles might understand this call they lead others in so much the better – and how much more clearly does His Rock now hear His voice!

> O Lord, when will we see you,
> when will we know you?
> We declare you our Lord and our God,
> but our thinking remains so earthly.
> Your Spirit impart to us
> that we might truly proclaim your divinity,
> and so, fully share in your Father's glory
> when you come with the holy angels.

Chapters of the Gospels

Chapter 9 – Transfiguration

On a high mountain Jesus is transfigured. Dazzlingly white become His clothes, He converses with Elijah and Moses… and the Father witnesses to His beloved Son. Here is a glimpse of the Lord's glory.

Then, down the mountain He comes to find a boy writhing on the ground and foaming at the mouth, deeply possessed by an unclean spirit. The pit could not be much darker. None can cure this troubled soul. But Jesus reaches His Spirit and His hand down to him to cast out the demon and raise the boy from the ground.

The Lord will die and He will rise. This is His teaching; this is the Word that confounds His disciples. How can one with such power over even death ever be killed? And what does it mean to rise from the dead?

In His transfiguration Jesus' resurrection is revealed, but all He can speak of is His crucifixion. Why? All He wishes for us is to remain humble, that pride might not take the kingdom from us. Better to lose hand or foot or eye than to be possessed by pride.

And do not the apostles tempt the fires of Gehenna when they discuss who is greatest among them? Would it not be better to be cast into the sea than to drink of this cup, than to be inflated by the leaven of the Pharisees? And so He sits a child in their midst, to show them how they must be.

If not humble, we shall never climb His mountain; exalting ourselves, we will be thrust to the ground. Though we walk in His company, He will not know us if our hearts do not serve the least of these, for then we will not be like Him.

Those who are of love are of love; those of peace are of peace. Every good deed done in the Name of the Lord will have its reward, and every sin its punishment. Let the fire of the Spirit burn in you if you wish to enter His glory.

> O Lord, we are not worthy to walk with you,
> or even to give your disciples a cup of water.
> Our faces should rather be to the ground
> than gazing upon your radiance.
> But embracing your Cross we are made whole,

and strength we find in you for doing good.
Let us serve you every day we toil on this plane.

Chapter 10 – Sacrificial Love

"Again crowds gathered around Him and, as was His custom, He again taught them." And all of what we hear in this chapter is contained in Matthew 19 and 20, but for rather minor variations. But in these deletions and additions, as well as in the drawing together of the material into one chapter, there is significance that is not negligible.

Here again Jesus speaks to the Pharisees and His disciples of the indissolubility of marriage, and here again the rich young man seeks eternal life. But since the Lord's touting of the celibate state is missing here, the sacredness of marriage is greater emphasized. He distinctly declares to the Pharisees and then the disciples that "what God has joined together, no human being must separate"; and then the transition to His blessing of the children is much more direct, much cleaner... and so the blessing of marriage is seen in an unfiltered light.

As for the story of the rich man (which I used previously to point up the call to religious life), we find here two very small but very important additions. By Mark we are told that Jesus, "looking at him, loved him," before He called the young man to sell everything he owned; and in speaking to Peter and the disciples of the blessings upon those who give up their lives for the kingdom, Jesus here adds that the "hundred times more" received in this age comes "with persecutions."

It is in love Jesus calls every soul to give his life for Him and the Gospel, because in this, eternal life is present even now – in this, Jesus, our Good God, is found. But who really wants to know Him and His love? For indeed that love comes with persecution, it comes with suffering... it requires the relinquishing of our many possessions, yes, but also the taking up of Christ's Cross.

Chapters of the Gospels

This the Lord makes clear in the second half of the chapter – material present in a separate chapter in Matthew. He speaks very forthrightly of the death that awaits Him in Jerusalem, giving details of the mockery, spitting, and scourging He will be made to endure. And then He emphasizes to John and James and the other apostles that His purpose is indeed "to give His life as a ransom for many," that He has "not come to be served but to serve," and that all who would follow Him must join in His sacrifice to know His glory.

This combining of the two chapters into one has produced an enlightening juxtaposition of the story of the rich man and that of blind Bartimaeus. Bartimaeus is, of course, he who (now one blind man, two in Matthew) begs by the side of the road, repeatedly calling out for pity as Jesus passes by. The young man approaches Bartimaeus' insistent desire in his running up and kneeling before the Lord to ask about eternal life, but how different he is upon receiving his answer.

In this is proven what Jesus states here and often of the obstacle riches are to finding the kingdom of God. For where the man of many possessions turns away from the Lord's loving invitation to join His company, the blind man upon receiving the sight for which he has petitioned hesitates not a moment in thankfully following Jesus on the road to Jerusalem.

Bartimaeus' readiness to leave all to be with the Son of David is exemplified in the fact that when called by the Lord, "he threw aside his cloak, sprang up, and came to Jesus." How much easier it is to set aside a single cloak than a multitude of possessions.

> O Lord, we are yours.
> Take all from us
> and let us realize your call.
> We sacrifice ourselves
> whether in married or religious life…
> Let us have no false gods before you.

Chapter 11 – Jesus' Entry

He has authority to cleanse the temple, driving out those who sell and buy there. He has power to cause the fig tree to wither or the mountain to be cast into the sea. He is worthy of the blessings the people cry out as He rides into Jerusalem on a colt. "Blessed is He who comes in the Name of the Lord!"

What is spoken of here is also in Matthew 21, though Matthew's chapter also contains the Parable of the Two Sons and the Parable of the Tenants (which is in the next chapter of Mark). Here the dramatic intensity of Jesus' entry into Jerusalem is blunted somewhat by His not cleansing the temple until the following day – and there is a day, too, between Jesus' cursing of the fig tree and its withering to its roots… but what is present here is almost entirely in Matthew.

But we think today not so much of Christ's deposing of the Pharisees from their place of power, as of the Lord's triumphal entry into each of our hearts to cleanse the temple that is our body and soul, that we might not wither to our roots at His command. To each of us He asks of our faith in John's baptism, and so in Himself; and each of us must answer with all the honesty we can muster.

Are we houses of prayer? Do we "have faith in God"? Do we believe that everything can be done in His Name – even the achievement of our own salvation – or do we question and doubt with the Pharisees? If the latter, we too will be deposed from our place in the heavenly kingdom, which the Lord comes now to prepare.

Let us continue to be "astounded at His teaching," in awe of His majestic presence, and all will be found with us exactly as He has promised – forgiving others we will be forgiven ourselves, and enter Jerusalem triumphantly with Him.

> O Lord, come to us and cleanse our hearts.
> Make your home within our souls,
> that we shall answer readily who you are.
> Find fruit upon these poor branches;
> early in the morning
> let us be blessed by you.

Chapters of the Gospels

Chapter 12 – Questions

A chapter of questions, some brought to Jesus to trap Him, others posed by the Lord to reveal Himself.

Again most of what is here is present in Matthew (spanning three chapters, but especially 22). Only the scribe's commendation of Jesus' answer to his question regarding the greatest commandment and His own commendation of the scribe, along with a short passage on the widow's mite, are new. But let us see what the Lord inspires in us in this reading.

Of the prophets Jesus says, "Some they beat, others they killed," and of His own murder He asks the Pharisees, "What then will the owner of the vineyard do?" He Himself gives the obvious answer, and so this cornerstone they seek to crush that it might not crush them… but they might as well try to throw a rope around the wind.

The Lord's brilliance is greatly in evidence here – in His tossing the coin back to His testers and calling them to give themselves to God, in His confounding any doubt about the resurrection and imparting a view of the kingdom to come, in His clear proclamation of the commandment to love, and ultimately in showing that David is indeed *His* son.

He is the Lord, there is no other. His wisdom cannot be gainsaid. He will quote you Scripture like it is written on His heart, for truly He is the Word of God. And He will look into every man's soul, and reveal what is written there. Who dare approach Him with question?

The chapter ends with a considerably shorter denunciation of the scribes, and tells of the poor widow. Does the Lord not see through "long robes" and the recitation of empty, "lengthy prayers"? Does He not recognize the love of a generous soul, she who gives all she owns? Will anything escape His vision?

There is none who will not be met by "the cornerstone" – the Son of the God of the living must be welcomed in our vineyard, and we must praise Him with every breath that is ours.

> O Lord, you are Lord.
> Son of God, you are our light.
> Dispel any question from our soul
> and teach us of your way in this world.

Let us be made in your image, dear Jesus,
and drink in the kingdom of the fruit of your vine.

Chapter 13 – Be Ready

(This chapter is substantially the same as Matthew 24, though again with relatively minor variations.)

"What stones and what buildings!" Yes, but what will become of these? What becomes of even the grandest structures of this world? Can anything remain? We know all shall be thrown down; by the Lord we have been told. Yes, "heaven and earth will pass away, but [His] words will not pass away."

And so, should we not listen to His words? Should we not heed what the eternal voice says? And what does He say? "Watch!" "Be alert!" The end is indeed near and He is at the door; can there be any still blind to the signs?

Yet He says, too, that we should "not be alarmed," that anxiety should not overtake us, lest we go after any who stand and claim to be the Messiah. There is none who knows the day or the hour of our visitation – *no one can say when the end will come.* Not even the Son! Only the Father in heaven holds such knowledge, and He is not walking amongst us on earth.

Be ready, yes, brothers and sisters. Be watchful; be prepared. But do not fear the tribulation. Be not deceived by "signs and wonders" false prophets proclaim. Even if made to suffer great persecution, believe always the Spirit is near, and that He will defend you in all adversity.

One interesting variation on the same text in Matthew is that here Jesus speaks only to Peter, James, John, and Andrew, rather than the disciples as a whole. It gives the discourse a much more intimate feel and a much more direct sense. Jesus perhaps speaks more quietly to these four principal apostles. He can more easily look each in the eye. There is a more private and profound and even reasoned air to instruction of a few.

Into our own souls the Lord's teaching must sink. We must listen to Him as He whispers His truth to our heart of hearts. The Lord

Chapters of the Gospels

allows us to overhear the words He imparts to those on the avant-garde of the kingdom to come; let us listen well to what we are privileged to be told.

> O Lord, let us be ready;
> let us be prepared at every moment.
> Whenever you break in upon us,
> let us greet you with shouts of joy.
> Yes, Lord, let us watch always for your coming.

Chapter 14 – Naked He Stands

A virtual mirror of Matthew 26. Little variation, though there are a few curious additions.

Here again we have the beginnings of the Passion of our Lord, and the events do parallel those in Matthew. I cannot help but think the recounting of these days and hours must have become very familiar to all the early Christians, in the strong oral tradition of the time – almost as if they were set in stone (which, of course, in a very real sense they are).

What strikes me now, aside from the variations I shall soon mention, is Jesus' anointing at Bethany by the woman with the "costly genuine spikenard." This preparation for burial seems very significant, and not just for the fact that His Passion is upon Him. Specifically, it comes before the Lord's Supper, when Jesus first offers Himself in the bloodless sacrifice of Holy Communion. Here He dies; here He must die if He is to offer Himself – is it not this death to which the woman's anointing of His body for burial applies?

There is here the detail of the cock crowing *two* times, adding a certain drama to Peter's denial. There is also the curious account of the young man "wearing nothing but a linen cloth about his body," who runs off naked when accosted in the Garden. (Could the linen signify the death the Lord Himself will throw off when He rises from the grave naked of this world?)

And there are also the fascinating details regarding Jesus' instructions to the disciples about where they should prepare the Passover. He tells them simply to follow a man carrying a jar of

Mark

water to the house where an upper room will be ready. It seems one of the more mystical (and mysterious) events of the Gospels.

Finally, we see more clearly here that "the spirit is willing but the flesh is weak," for in addition to the principal apostles' inability to keep their eyes open despite the Lord's repeated entreaties for their prayers at a critical moment of His life (and of all time), we also are told (twice) that Peter was "warming himself at the fire" in the courtyard of the high priest as Jesus was being interrogated – and condemned – inside, indicating that the Rock of the Church could not bear the cold air all around him. (Satan will indeed use the weakness of our flesh to break down our defenses.)

Our Savior enters upon His Passion as His sheep disperse. Naked He stands before His accusers, and naked He shall die. But we will be clothed with everlasting life.

> O Lord, forgive our betrayal of your love.
> We are weak, as you know.
> We wish you needn't have suffered for our sins,
> but now please let us walk with you…
> By your grace let us never deny you.

Chapter 15 – Forsaken

The Passion of Jesus from condemnation to burial, as in Matthew 27 – though with fewer details. The only two details peculiar to Mark are the people's initiative in asking Pilate to keep to his policy of releasing a prisoner for them at Passover, and that Pilate was "amazed" Jesus had already died when Joseph came for His body.

Were the people going to ask that Jesus be released before the chief priests stirred up the crowd to call for Barabbas instead (and to have our Savior crucified)? It would seem so from the text. It would thus show a lack of genuine resolve on the part of the Jews that the Christ be crucified, which would account for many repenting after His resurrection and specifically at Pentecost.

That crucifixion would not ordinarily cause death within a few hours is evident from Pilate's reaction. Much longer were criminals usually displayed and made to suffer. Perhaps it can be surmised

Chapters of the Gospels

from this that it was not so much the nails and a loss of blood that killed the Redeemer, but His great anguish at seeing those whom He loved (and remember, He loves every soul) go so far against the will of God.

When He cries out, "My God, my God, why have you forsaken me?" it is not His own pain or even His own desolation that He laments – He looks out at all who abuse Him (including the two souls crucified with Him), sees how far from the love of God they are, takes their sins and their desolation upon Himself... and cries out for mercy upon our wayward race.

> Come to us, O God!
> Leave us not alone in our rebellion.
> Hide not your face from us,
> despite our sins.
> See how your Son has suffered,
> how He has answered for our lack of love...
> and may His death be pleasing to you,
> and may we no longer be imprisoned
> for our crimes against your grace.
> May the death we deserve
> be taken from us
> by the death He has endured in our stead.

Chapter 16 – The Great Commission

At sunrise on the first day, the women rush to the tomb carrying the spices they've bought to prepare the corpse of the Lord. But their spices will not be necessary.

Neither do they need to wonder who will roll back the stone from the tomb for them, for an angel has taken care of that.

Jesus is risen! He is not where they laid Him. All will see Him.

But here (in the longer ending) we have the 'doubting Eleven' instead of just doubting Thomas, for it is recorded that none believed the reports of Mary Magdalene or the two disciples who had been walking along on their way to the country, to whom the Lord had appeared. Here Jesus rebukes all eleven for their unbelief before commissioning them to go forth in His Name preaching the Gospel to every creature throughout the whole world.

I suppose one must know one's own doubt before one can cure the doubt of another. And it is to faith, to healing, the apostles call all souls. Let all come to the eternal salvation won by the Lord!

> O Jesus, you are with us yet in your disciples;
> you work through the hands of those you send.
> Let us put faith in them
> and so in you,
> that we might be healed of all sin
> and come to the glory of your resurrection.
> Amen.

Chapters of the Gospels

III.

The Gospel of Luke

Chapter 1 – Light Breaks In

God is faithful and merciful! He has brought salvation to His people! The word of the holy prophets is fulfilled – Jesus, the Son of the Most High, is conceived in the womb of the Virgin, and John the Baptist is born to hail His coming.

Here the light of God breaks into human history. Here the angel of the Lord, Gabriel, brings the message of joy to Zechariah – that his aged wife shall bear him a son – and the most wonderful, awe-inspiring message of all to Mary: that of her will be born the Son of God.

Who would not be fearful at such proclamation? Who could bear to hear what the human heart could not conceive? After so many years, so many centuries of darkness, of longing, of waiting… light indeed breaks into our midst. The covenant with Abraham and with David will finally be fulfilled. A new age dawns upon God's chosen ones.

The circumstances surrounding the birth of John are indeed remarkable: the angel's appearance, his unbelievable message, Zechariah's inability to speak, the child's name, and then the opening of the old priest's mouth at his acceptance of the name – at the acceptance of this servant of Israel (caretaker of the covenant of old) of the grace of God, of this new thing occurring in his midst… and his marvelous canticle inspired by the Holy Spirit.

But more wonderful still is the angel's overwhelming word to the poor young virgin. Who could believe such a thing? Who is it that speaks it to her? This word must utterly empty her soul of any other thought, of any other word, in order to find place to take root. (How could she contain such a Word if not prepared beforehand by God?) Nothing of the world, no sin, no darkness, could be in her if she is to accept into her womb the God made Man, if she is to conceive by the power of the Holy Spirit.

One can only be astounded, can only be made speechless himself, if he listens well to the account Luke offers. To believe such events is to be upon redemption itself. Can you hear the Spirit speaking through Elizabeth, through Mary, through Zechariah? Do their songs touch your heart and raise it up to the throne of God, where your

Luke

Savior sits even this hour? Can you bear the Holy Spirit's fire? Let His voice raise you from your lowliness, from the dust you are, to gaze upon the wonders of the Lord.

> O Holy Spirit, overshadow us with God's grace.
> Bring the light of the Lord to this dark place
> that has languished so long
> in expectation of the promise fulfilled,
> that our hearts, too, might leap with joy
> at your voice touching our muted ears and tongues.
> Open the curtains of time to let in this ray,
> to let Jesus into our souls through the Blessed Virgin…
> that we all might wonder at the greatness of the Father's love
> made known now in our midst
> and removing all reproach from us.

Chapter 2 – A Child Is Born

The marvels continue and the people continue to be amazed at the movement of the Holy Spirit in the birth of our Savior, at the angel's proclamation of this Good News to the shepherds in the field, and then at the appearance of the multitude singing and praising God. Here lying in a simple manger is a little child wrapped in swaddling clothes – what could be more ordinary, yet what could be more marvelous? The word of the angel is fulfilled before the shepherds' eyes: here is the Messiah, the Son of God!

And the marvels continue as the Child Jesus is presented in the temple and two aged prophets, Simeon and Anna, declare openly the absolute blessing this Child, the Savior, is for all peoples. Here is "a light for revelation to the Gentiles, and glory for [God's] people Israel."

Here the Spirit indeed moves and speaks: Simon utters his blessing upon the Holy Family, raising Jesus in his arms while blessing God as well for this "sign of contradiction" that will reveal the thoughts of many hearts, whose own heart a sword shall pierce, as even it does His Mother's.

Then the Spirit speaks through Jesus Himself as He is found in the temple with the teachers of the people. Astounded once more are all who hear what the Spirit says through this twelve-year-old boy. For His questions are probing and revelatory (as later they shall fully be) and every answer in wisdom He seems to possess.

Of course, He must be found in the temple – where else but where God dwells? For the Father lives in Him and He in the Father, and nowhere apart from the Father could He ever be.

Do not wonder any longer, brothers and sisters. Do not question what these things mean. Mary now knows and you are now told: here is the Son of God who has come to full wisdom in our presence.

Alleluia! we must sing, joining with the choir of angels; for to heaven now all are called, with their glorious number. Shepherds and prophets and mother and father and all the souls who have ears now hear the wondrous voice of the Spirit speaking in the flesh of our Savior. Alleluia! Let us go in peace into His presence.

> In your Temple let us ever dwell, O LORD,
> in the flesh of your only Son.
> The Holy Spirit be upon us now
> to open our hearts to the Word among us.
> Let us glorify and praise you, O God,
> for your consolation toward us.
> Let us, too, become strong and wise…
> let your favor be upon us.

Chapter 3 – The Voice in the Wilderness

Luke is particularly precise in placing John the Baptist and his time of preaching, as well as the coming of the Lord, in human history. He tells us the names of the rulers at the time of John's call to repentance and traces the generations leading to Jesus (through Joseph) all the way back to Adam – and so to God and Creation itself! (Quite a remarkable offering from the good physician who has looked so carefully into matters surrounding the Christ.)

He is also more detailed in his explanation of the message John proclaimed to the people, quoting his words to the crowds in general

Luke

(i.e. share food and clothes with others) and specifically to tax collectors and soldiers – neither of whom he counsels to leave their posts, but rather to be honest about their work.

And so, even stronger does John's exhortation seem because of these details. Adding to the intensity is the fact that he calls not only the scribes and Pharisees a "brood of vipers" but *everyone*, thus getting across the point that the need for repentance is urgent for all of us, not just some few notable sinners. The Messiah is coming and even John himself, the great voice in the wilderness preparing His way, is "not worthy to loosen the thongs of His sandals." Can any soul then put off repentance?

Jesus is baptized, too. The Spirit descends upon Him, as it does no other. The fire of the beloved Son is upon mankind – let us make straight the way of the Lord while we yet have time.

> O Lord, you are with us now,
> having stepped into human history.
> Your word has been duly proclaimed
> and all are called into your presence.
> May the fire of your love burn away all our sins.
> Let us heed the exhortation upon our souls.

Chapter 4 – His Power and Authority

He who refuses to bow down to the devil is praised by all for His power and His authority. He has come "to proclaim a year acceptable to the Lord," to fulfill Scripture in the sight and hearing of the people.

And they see. And they hear. They see the marvels He performs before their eyes, curing souls of unclean spirits and various diseases; and they hear the truth, the "gracious words" issuing from His mouth... and none can deny the authority with which He speaks and acts.

And yet He must rebuke. Certainly He must rebuke fevers and demons as He brings sacred healing, and certainly the devil must be rebuked in his vain temptations – but His townspeople, too, must be rebuked for their faithlessness... as we all must be rebuked if we are to gain salvation.

Chapters of the Gospels

But let us pray our reaction is not like those in Nazareth, for when told Elijah went to no widow of Israel and Elisha cured no leper of the Chosen race – and so that they will not know Him whom the LORD has sent – in fury they attempt to accomplish what the devil himself has failed to do: though Jesus refused to cast Himself down from the parapet of the temple (the last temptation recorded by Luke, Satan's sort of final effort to kill Him whom he could not conquer), those in His native place would have hurled Him down headlong from the brow of the hill of their town by their own murderous hands.

But in Capernaum He is gratefully accepted – let us imitate them. They come from everywhere as news spreads of His power. They would not let Him leave their town, and search Him down to bring Him back… But on He must go, to be accepted or rejected in other towns, in all towns, as in all hearts. And so, after a respite alone in a deserted place, it is time for Him to move on.

> Begone, Satan, we shall not fall to your tests.
> God alone we shall worship,
> for He alone feeds our souls.
> We shall not die,
> for our Lord does live
> and He has conquered you and all your kind.
> Jesus, in your word and in your flesh
> we make our home –
> let us never leave you.

Chapter 5 – His Saving Net

Let all sinners come to Jesus on their knees, begging His forgiveness. Like the leper prostrate before Him, pleading to be made clean; like Peter at the knees of our Savior, saying, "Depart from me, for I am a sinful man"; like the paralytic lowered to the feet of the Lord; like all the tax collectors and others whose sin is known… let us answer His call to repentance. For He is in our midst, and should we not rejoice?

Luke

Make your hearts new, brothers and sisters, to receive His grace and mercy; harden them not against the glory revealed in the Son. It is to His wedding feast He now calls all sinners, that we might be redeemed by Him.

And like Peter and James and John, like Matthew and all the apostles of the Lord, we are called to be fishers of men. All souls He would gather into His skin to share the wine of new life – let wholeness and healing come upon everyone this day!

Through Peter, the Lord brings His salvation forth. In the boat of this Rock of the Church all fish are gathered. Even if they are to fill the boat of the sons of Zebedee and the boats of apostles around the world, still it is Peter by whom they are caught; it is his nets that are primarily blessed by the Christ.

But let healing go out to all this day; murmur not at the grace being poured forth. For the Bridegroom is near and the table of the feast is even now being laid. Let none fail to bring their sickness to Him, that all might be struck with amazement at the wonders Jesus performs.

> O Lord, may our leprosy leave us immediately;
> may we not hesitate to follow where you go.
> We have heard of the glory of your presence
> and pray now we too shall rise and go forth.
> Our hearts let be set upon your blessed call
> that we might enter freely into the kingdom's hall.
> Alleluia! Alleluia! Alleluia!

Chapter 6 – Love Thy Enemy

Why is it Jesus' goodness engenders such rage? Why does His great mercy bring great persecution? Why does His way lead to crucifixion?

Why all hearts do not turn in joy to the Lord's loving call can only be attributed to the sin of man, to his stubborn disobedience in the face of undeniable truth. And because of the evil in men's hearts, with Christ we are made to suffer; our goodness can only be treated as has the Lord's own.

Chapters of the Gospels

If in hatred tongues turn upon us, if hands are raised to strike us down, it cannot be that we return in kind the treatment tendered, nor can we cease to walk Christ's path.

There is no choice for us who would call Him Savior; if He is our Lord, we must be as He is. For if we fail to act upon the truth He teaches, if the love He generously offers we spurn in blindness or inertia… what shall bring us to the kingdom of God?

We cannot judge even those who hate us. We cannot condemn the worst sinner to the pit. Salvation only Jesus brings; we cannot afford to take else upon ourselves, or we too will be blind.

From a level stretch upon the mountain Jesus teaches; plain to our hearts He makes His lofty commands. Such mercy bleeds in all Christ's disciples, all who are sent to love as the Twelve.

And so, healing follows in our wake now; the goodness of God cannot be stopped. Though they take our possessions and even kill us, our love for all souls will never rot. And thus, living such love we will stand strong on the Day of our God.

Luke adds eternal woes to Jesus' blessings, the woes of those who reject His call. Let us not be found among them, but rather eating bread at the Lord's hand, keeping in mind – our weeping now is temporary; the weeping then will have no end.

> O Lord, how your sweet Cross
> fills the waiting soul with joy;
> how your dying brings great life
> to your disciples.
> Let your blood pour upon us for healing,
> that seeing your goodness abound,
> we might also bear fruit with you…
> leading the blind to your house.

Chapter 7 – The Blind See

"The blind regain their sight, the lame walk, lepers are cleansed, the deaf hear, the dead are raised, the poor have the Good News proclaimed to them." And who could take offense at such wonders?

Luke

Certainly not the centurion whose favored slave is saved from his deathbed. Certainly not the widow whose only son is raised from his bier. Certainly not the woman whose many sins are pardoned. All who know the healing grace that pours forth from the Son of God can only rejoice, as do the crowds that surround them.

But what about certain of the Pharisees who look askance at such marvels, who begrudge the woman her freedom from Satan's clutches, who are not satisfied unless the Lord dances to their tune and weeps to their dirge? These judge the ways of Jesus as unsuitable to themselves, and so end in condemnation. Of all the words of Scripture, can there be sadder than these about the Pharisees and scholars of the law: "[They] rejected the plan of God for themselves"? And so by their own plans they die.

John is assured of Jesus' divinity by all he hears of the Savior's deeds. The witness of his messengers is enough to set his heart at ease here at the end of his days. That such wonders are worked is enough sign to him that the Holy One has come, for he is a man of faith.

A man of faith is the centurion as well, though not born into the people of God. His faith and humility are underscored in Luke by his not coming to the Lord himself to beg his servant's healing but sending, first, elders of the Jews (there are some of these of faith, you see), then his friends, to speak with the one true Savior. He knows his messengers will fulfill his task – as even the words they deliver attest – and not only does he deem himself unworthy for Jesus to come under his roof, but unworthy even to appear before Him. (Indeed, where is such reverence shown in any other man?)

> O Lord, may we in faith and humility
> come to you
> or simply beg your saints to intercede…
> for your forgiveness we certainly need;
> your healing every wise soul ardently seeks.
> As we weep at your feet,
> hear our cry,
> and let us witness your marvels in our life.

Chapters of the Gospels
Chapter 8 – Broken Chains

As a large crowd gathers before Him from one town after another, Jesus proclaims the parable of the sower. Indeed, God's Word does not find reception in every heart, for many are deaf or waste the grace the Son of Man offers. Few will persevere and produce mature fruit.

Nothing is hidden from the light of the Lord; it exposes the secrets of every soul. That you hear the Word of God will be known by your actions – only by your fruit will you become His kin.

All must be healed, first of all, and healed by faith. Like the women who followed Jesus and provided for Him and His disciples out of their means, first the demons must be cast from us. Like the demoniac of Geresene, we must first be made whole before we can proclaim what the Lord has done for us. And as with the woman with the hemorrhage and the official of the synagogue (Jairus), we cannot be saved from our infirmity or see our daughter raised unless we have faith.

There is an abyss which even the demons seek to avoid, which the disciples fear upon them as the squall blows over their boat, into which Jairus' daughter seems to all to have descended and from which all would long to be saved.

But we need not be seized with fear of the Savior lifting us from there. We should not be so acceptant of the darkness that surrounds us that its dispersion we fear even more so! For the Lord's light we must thirst, and maintain such desire within us; for He will come and break any shackle that holds us, and draw us into His kingdom.

Only make room for His Word in your heart, and have faith. Your redemption is at hand.

> O may the crowds of souls that surround you, Lord,
> truly reach out and touch your love,
> for so many can seem so close
> yet remain at a fearful distance.
> In your company let us truly be,
> your Word growing ever in our hearts,
> that like your Mother we may serve you well
> and flesh of your flesh become.
> Food from your tree let us eat.

Luke

Chapter 9 – The Exodus

In the glorious light of Jesus' transfiguration, Moses and Elijah speak of the exodus the Lord is about to accomplish in Jerusalem. The only way out of this world of darkness to the glory of God is by the Cross – Jesus makes this eminently clear.

Great marvels are performed here in this chapter, by God the Father, by Jesus the Son, and by His disciples. The great majesty of the Lord is revealed in the healing of diseases and the casting out of demons, in the feeding of five thousand, and in the voice from a cloud of heaven; but the sharp nail of Jesus' rebuke pierces through all and fixes His call to the Cross.

"Pay attention to what I am telling you," Jesus insists, repeating that the Son must die. To heaven would His disciples fly – but He must keep the Cross before their eyes.

There is no tent on earth to hold the glory of God: "the Son of Man has nowhere to rest His head." And so do not become enamored of any wonder you may glimpse, for it is not in this you are to make your home. All must be left behind; all must die. Do not cling to anything of earth, but "let the dead bury their dead" – you are called to life in heaven.

The ruler of this world is perplexed, as are all of this "faithless and perverse generation." Jesus will not long be upon this corrupted plane; heed His rebuke while such grace is with you. Be not ashamed of Him or His words, lest in His glory He be ashamed of you.

The end is very near. It cannot be otherwise, for the Messiah of God has come. Here His disciples but shake the dust from their feet in testimony against the souls that reject them; yet do they move on to the next town. But, though no fire be called down to destroy the wicked at this time… the fire is prepared for the end of time. Those not humble as a child threaten the consuming fire not far from any man.

Leave behind all things else to follow Him, and the Lord's fire will purge you now of your sin, that you might be redeemed for His kingdom.

Chapters of the Gospels

> O Lord, in groups of fifty let us sit,
> patiently waiting for the food at your hands;
> like the child you set beside yourself,
> let our soul find a home with you.
> Your Word pierce our hearts
> that they may be as your own,
> that bled of corruption we may stand
> and enter gratefully the glory of heaven...
> where all things we shall comprehend.

Chapter 10 – "Go and Do Likewise"

This chapter begins in similar fashion to the previous – here, rather than the Twelve apostles, Jesus sends seventy-two disciples with "no money bag, no sack, no sandals," to cure the sick and announce the kingdom of God at hand. And so the mission spreads wider as the Lord's time draws nigh. "Peace" is what all those He sends declare. They stand in His place now: will we accept or reject the words of God's Church?

Jesus has "observed Satan fall like lightning from the sky," and so He gives "the power 'to tread upon serpents' and scorpions" to all of faith who come like children with eyes open wide to the Lord's love and truth. And nothing there is not subject to such trust.

But that faith must be maintained and that love put into practice. Only loving God and neighbor will we retain our discipleship; else we shall be like the rebellious towns which Jesus condemns. The scholar, wishing to justify himself, asked the Lord, "Who is my neighbor?" – whom should he love? – but because of his impertinence we now see clearly whom and how we are to love.

It is in Luke alone the parable of the Good Samaritan appears (along with the story of the burdened Martha and the prayerful Mary). It is one of those most commonly known. Yet, do we put into practice the Samaritan's compassion? Or are we still like the priest and the Levite, avoiding those in need?

All are our brothers and sisters. This may seem a vain platitude, but nothing is more true... and nothing more difficult to comprehend. Only by looking at Jesus' arms spread upon the Cross do we come to realize what it means to love every other man. It is to just such love as only the Savior possesses He calls us this day, saying, "Go and do likewise" for your neighbor.

But be not so concerned for the plight of your brother that you lose sight of God beside you, for without His love your serving will be futile. The first and better part is always the love of God; if truly you love Him and listen closely to His words, already your love for your neighbor will have begun.

> O blessed are our eyes, O Lord,
> for it is you they see;
> blessed our ears,
> for by your words they are fed.
> Inspire us, O Lord, with your blessed call –
> send us out as laborers into your harvest.
> Let us listen to your Church as in it you speak,
> and so find even this day the kingdom of God.
> We love you, O Lord; let our love be known.

Chapter 11 – Blessed Instruction

Jesus has chastising words for the scribes and Pharisees, and all those who speak against the Spirit of God working through Him, those who fail to repent at His preaching. But He also gives blessed instruction about prayer.

"Ask and you will receive; seek and you will find; knock and the door will be open to you." Indeed, these words soar as if on wings of doves, calling us all to union with God. The Father loves us and hears our prayers; He is not remiss in providing for our needs. He would give us our daily bread if we would but ask. But who is there that asks? Who is there with faith that God listens? And who genuinely seeks the forgiveness of his sins while forgiving others?

The Father loves us so much He has sent His Son to call all souls to recognize their sins, that His great love and mercy might be known in our lives by the power of the Holy Spirit. But who can bear Christ's chastising word? Do we not rather rebel against Him like the scribes and Pharisees as He exposes our faults one by one?

Chapters of the Gospels

The Lord has come to cast Satan from our presence by the power of the fire that is in Him. From our souls and bodies He would take all darkness, that we might be filled with light and shine His glory for all to see. But too many turn away from His grace. And these will be found with blood on their hands.

The blood of the prophets is filled up in the crucifixion of Jesus, and those who kill Him are as graves themselves. Their darkness is unending, deeper than any pit on earth. To turn from His blessing is to give a snake to the Son... and from the final test these shall not be saved.

> O the woe of all souls
> who harden their hearts against you, Lord,
> who do not immerse themselves in your blessed wisdom.
> For only you hold light;
> apart from you, we are as unseen graves –
> into such darkness let us not fall.
> But rather let your kingdom come
> to each of your faithful children.
> Hear our prayer this day.

Chapter 12 – God's Kingdom Alone

Jesus has come to set the earth on fire, to be a cause of division among souls, that the thoughts of all hearts might be exposed to the light, that truth might be known and all who hold to it be gathered into His house and invited to recline at His table.

Can you not interpret the present time, my brothers and sisters? Neither wind nor rain, nor clothes nor food, nor anything else of this earth has meaning – it is all as grass that will be tossed into the fire. God's kingdom alone matters, for only it is lasting, and only His food satisfies.

You are called while here to witness to the Christ, to acknowledge the Son of Man before others. If you do not do so, then you hide the truth and therefore partake of hypocrisy. This is not the food you are meant to eat or to share with others of your kind.

Luke

Though it bring persecution, you must proclaim the word of God from the housetops; you must entrust yourself to the Lord and allow Him to speak and to work through you. If your heart is set rather on the riches of this world, then there is nothing for you but to die this night. For if empty of the Spirit of truth, we are empty of life; and when greed enters in, we are eaten away from the inside.

Nothing escapes "the notice of God." He sees all and hears all and knows all. To think to fool Him is to invite condemnation upon yourself. For He does not delay and will not be long in coming. You had better settle with Him now along the way; you had better do His will day to day, not wasting a moment on darkness, on the dereliction of your duty toward Him… or He will come at an unknown time, and punishment alone you will own.

> O Lord, though your light be harsh
> to our corrupted hearts and minds,
> though the baptism you bring
> be painful to our faithless souls,
> yet come, dear Lord,
> and take us into your hand,
> cradling us in your palm
> as the merest sparrow.

Chapter 13 – The Narrow Gate

The Lord would lead us all through the narrow gate, for it is the narrow gate that leads to heaven, and all from north and south, east and west, He would have enter the kingdom of God. But who will persevere in this way?

A year of favor is upon us. Jesus comes to set us free from all our infirmities that we might stand erect with the dignity with which the Father has endowed us as His blessed children. But if we do not cultivate and fertilize our ground, if we do not repent of our sins, this year of favor will pass us by and we shall be left abandoned on the road – or have a tower fall upon our heads.

It is so, that the Lord would see none perish. It is thus that He continues unwaveringly along the path that leads to His crucifixion in the chosen city of Jerusalem. He will bleed for us, He will die for us, but He cannot gather us into His arms if we are unwilling – for we *are* children of God, made in His image, and the freedom that characterizes the Creator of all is indelibly marked in our souls… and so we must choose our redemption.

The crowd rejoices as Jesus humbles the Pharisees who protest the healing of the crippled woman on the Sabbath. They become exuberant at "the splendid deeds done by Him." All well and good. But the Savior cautions them and us that as marvelous as such miracles of God may be, it is our obedience and our patient endurance He values above all. Heaven is not a plant that shoots up overnight, for these but die the following day. Rather, the kingdom of God grows gradually, imperceptibly, in those committed to the narrow way.

And so, do not take for granted the Messiah's graces; do not presume His salvation upon your soul. Each day you must repent of your sins to find yourself one step closer to the kingdom of God.

> O Lord, let us not end in disaster!
> Vigilant make us of your coming presence.
> This day let us repent and believe,
> and so draw near to your blessed table.

Chapter 14 – The Wedding Feast

"Everything is now ready." The Lord is inviting you to His kingdom, to the wedding feast of the righteous. Have you some more pressing matter to attend to than the salvation of your eternal soul?

It is the Sabbath day, the day of rest and feasting; it is the promised hour. Now the Lord would bless you; now He would seat you at His table. But you must be ready to build this tower that reaches to the heavens – you must be prepared to fight the good fight against all odds. You can only do this if you realize He is with you to heal your every weakness, to pull you from any pit into which you may fall.

A most distinguished guest is in our midst. He has entered our race and come to sit at our table in this humble place. And He is meet

Luke

to the call. He does not presume to take the higher position but empties Himself of all majesty to be beside us in all things. And are we like Him? Or do our proud souls assume a standing that is not our own, one to which only our Savior can call us?

Do not excuse yourself from the severity of His call. Do not look to that which is easier to accomplish or which seems more fulfilling at the moment. There is no greater grace than to be Jesus' disciple, for as the master so does the student become – renounce all else that this blessing you may know. All of this world is but a fleeting shadow, and all must be placed at the service of God.

See that your salt not lose its savor. See that from your life your faith be not taken, or you will be left empty and dry and find no holy ground into which to lay your body, and find your life does not cause the kingdom's fruits to increase and multiply.

> Humble let us be before you, Lord,
> and before one another,
> and you will raise us from the dust
> and heal our dropsy.
> And to your feast we will be invited
> with the poor and the crippled,
> the lame and the blind…
> with all those your love looks upon.

Chapter 15 – God's Mercy

A chapter of mercy, of the compassion of God, and of the reconciliation of His two sons.

How great is the love of our Father for *all* His children, whether they dissipate His property or complain of their brother's indigence. Whether we be profligate or jealous, the Lord loves us still. Every sinner He seeks out.

Three parables – the Lost Sheep, the Lost Coin, and the Lost Son – each illustrating what joy the Lord takes in finding us present in His House. Though ninety-nine of a hundred remain faithful, yet He longs for that one soul to turn, that He might lift him onto His shoulders toward heaven, where the angels of God rejoice. In every dark corner He searches for us, calling us from the hell we make. His eyes are ever looking down the road for our return. (Do you hear His heart beating for you even now?)

The Parable of the Prodigal Son is, of course, the epitome of God's great love for us. Reading it carefully can but bring one to tears. For who has not felt himself removed from God's presence, alone as if in a strange town? Who has not been foolish about his stewardship of the Lord's gifts and talents – who has not thought the Father's face would be turned away from him?

And who has not judged his brother? Who has not questioned God's gracious blessings upon some undeserving soul, and wondered why such blessings were not his own?

The parables are primarily addressed to the scribes and Pharisees, who cannot comprehend Jesus' association with sinful men. Often we hear in the Gospels the Savior's recounting of the woes upon these vain and judgmental souls, and this in the harshest words. But here the teaching is of a different kind: here there is acknowledgment of the closeness of these leaders of the people to the Father God.

First, Jesus reminds the scribes and Pharisees of their own concern for members of their flock, as if to ask if the Lord should be less caring than they. If men rejoice over finding a sheep or a coin, should not the Father find greater joy in discovering a lost child and bringing him into His fold?

But the Lord's love for those who sit on Moses' seat is all the more apparent in Jesus' quotation of the father's words to his elder son: "My son, you are here with me always; everything I have is yours." The older son is undoubtedly an image for the Pharisees, who keep so well to the law, and Jesus almost certainly speaks the above quote directly into their eyes, to their heart, calling them to love the brother He is beckoning back into the Father's arms.

> O Lord, let us celebrate and rejoice
> over every lost sinner that has been found by you.
> Let us join the angels and the saints
> in their joy for each soul entering the heavenly fold.
> But let us thank you, most of all,
> that you have redeemed *us* from our prisons...
> Your mercy is boundless – let it pour upon all.

Luke

Chapter 16 – Wise Stewardship

What are we to do with the wealth that comes to us in this dark world? Are we to fat ourselves with sumptuous foods and parade around in fine clothing? If we do so, we but prepare ourselves for torment in the flames of hell.

Rather, we are to utilize such riches wisely, for the upbuilding of the kingdom of heaven, for the care of those in need. We must not allow Lazarus to lie at our doorstep starving while we have the means to alleviate his suffering. For ultimately it will be we who suffer, as he is gathered into the Lord's arms.

We have a duty, a call from our Lord – a work to be accomplished even in this world. If we do not use well what is at our hands, we shall be responsible. Though this be earth and not heaven, we cannot abandon ourselves to *its* beck and call. It is not our appetites we must satisfy but the Lord's desires for all His children, for all His kingdom.

Use the decaying matter of this world, the passing things of this passing universe, to proclaim the love of God, and you will have proven yourself worthy to enter His eternal presence. Do not drown in the mammon of this empty life.

In this chapter also, Jesus makes clear that there is no divide between the teaching of the law and the prophets and His own, when He states, "If they will not listen to Moses and the prophets, neither will they be persuaded if someone should rise from the dead." Though His death and resurrection fulfill the word of old, there is nothing essentially new or different about the Word the Lord now brings… and not a letter of the law is made invalid as by the Savior's grace each word is brought to fullness and light. (Are our hearts open to listen and heed the call of the ages upon our soul?)

> O Lord, let us follow you into the heavenly kingdom.
> As you humbled yourself to walk this earth
> and proclaimed God's favor with every action and word,
> let us, too, put all that we own
> at the service of Almighty God.
> Make us wise in our dealings here
> that to eternal dwellings we may be welcomed.

Chapters of the Gospels
Chapter 17 – Humble Faith

Of faith and a disciple's preparation for the kingdom.

Of faith: it is clear that the Lord associates faith with the virtues of humility and gratitude. When the apostles ask Him to increase their faith, He speaks of a mustard seed, the smallest of seeds, to indicate that faith, though it accomplish tremendous deeds, is but tiny itself, is found in the man who makes himself humble; for it is then he knows the grandeur of God, who alone accomplishes all. (I would say God is more humble than a speck of dust because His humility surpasses any image of this world.)

The Lord also speaks to them here of being but an obedient servant, emphasizing, of course, that it is really God who does everything good, not us; but also, certainly, just how humble a man of faith must be – he must be as nothing. And then he will be like God. For who has come to serve more so than Jesus the Son? Who is more humble than the Great One?

This connection between faith and humility, and gratitude (for the servant is also grateful just for being blessed to serve), is brought out in the story of the ten lepers as well. It is when the cleansed Samaritan leper returns glorifying God and falling at the feet of Jesus in thanksgiving that the Lord commends him for his faith. (Who among us knows the grateful place we find face down to the ground before Jesus? Who is there of genuine faith?)

And of our preparation for the coming kingdom: certainly we must have faith. And that faith must realize in what measure the kingdom is already in our midst, that Jesus has already come and left His Spirit, in order to be ready for the kingdom's final coming, for Jesus' return in glory.

We will not find the kingdom if we do not know it now. If our hearts are rather set on the food and drink of this earth, how will we come to the table of the Lord (which He sets before us even this day at Holy Mass)? If we take our pleasure in this place, it is in this place we shall end, the vultures picking at our flesh.

Do not proudly look about yourself, predicting the Savior's return. Fire and brimstone will surely come, and even now are prepared to fall. Look at your heart and see that it is not like that of the wife of

Lot: is it ready to leave all of this world behind, or does it look back upon some temptation present in this life?

Repent while there is time, and encourage your brother to do the same. For it will not be long till one is taken and another left; and then you may regret that you did not now find your faith in the hand of God.

> O Lord, let us but serve you this day.
> As all things pass away,
> let our hearts be set upon your presence.
> We thank you for all you have done for us;
> complete your work in us when you come again.
> Till then may we be your worthless servants,
> doing only what you command us to do.

Chapter 18 – Like a Child

"Accept the kingdom of God like a child"; come humbly before the Lord, your head bowed, beating your breast; "sell all that you have," and give it to the poor; remain persistent in your prayer, calling out to the Lord… and indeed the kingdom will be yours.

A child of God owns nothing of this world – all his cares are in the hands of his heavenly Father. And a child's faith does not waver, for it knows nothing of the devil's distractions but is set on one purpose: to walk with its Savior on the road to Jerusalem.

There is a marvelous framing to this chapter, with the parable of the persistent widow at its beginning and the healing of the blind beggar at its end. In the first, Jesus enjoins us to "call out to [God] day and night," that He will certainly hear and answer quickly – He will render a just decision more surely than any judge. And in the last, the Lord's teaching is proven true, as the blind man persists in shouting to the Son of David, despite the crowd's ordering him to silence and Jesus' seeming to continue on His way. The Lord does stop, He does inquire as to the man's desire… and He does heal him immediately.

Chapters of the Gospels

In the middle of the chapter, the dangers of riches are recounted for us once again. But there are riches more than wealth of possessions that will prevent our entering God's kingdom – here the Pharisees' pride is shown to be as great an obstacle to going home justified. Yes, if we exalt ourselves, remembering our virtues but forgetting the vices to which the eyes of God are not blind, then humbled shall we indeed be. But remembering that we are sinners, humble creatures of our Father God, the Lord will pity us and raise us on high. (Thus like a child we must come to our Savior.)

Finally, as Jesus speaks openly of His impending Passion, we are told that the Twelve "understood nothing." Utterly uncomprehending are these leaders of His Church of the essence of the call they must find in Christ. But, yes, the Spirit will come and open their eyes.

> We are nothing but blind, O Lord.
> Our vision is so faulty,
> with trouble only we see even what is before us.
> Let us repent, let us pray,
> let us call upon your Name…
> let us come as children to your loving touch,
> and our cross will be light
> as it leads us to heaven.

Chapter 19 – He Wept

Jesus approaches Jerusalem, but He stops to stay at the house of a sinner and to teach us of our call in His wake. He laments over Jerusalem and her imminent destruction, but He enters the temple to purge it of sin.

Why should the Lord stop at the house of a sinner even as He nears the holy city, where the people expect the kingdom of God to appear? Why should He care for a man so short in moral stature as the chief tax collector Zacchaeus? Does it not show clearly that "the Son of Man has come to seek and save the lost," that His eyes and arms are always open to find a repentant heart?

Luke

And Zacchaeus does not disappoint. He declares half of his possessions shall go to the poor and he shall make good four times over to anyone he has cheated. Was it not worth the Lord's time to make this stop along His way? (Do not forget that He will treat each one of us just the same.)

And the parable of the ten gold coins makes clear indeed our call to serve the Lord here now as His faithful disciples. He is going away and His kingdom will not come immediately, but, though His fellow citizens despise Him and reject Him as their king – as even the priests and scribes and other leaders do upon His entry into Jerusalem, seeking even to put Him to death – still He leaves with each of us a measure of His possessions, a coin we must employ, that we might receive His blessing upon His return. Yes, as those who have rebelled against Him are slain before Him, those who have been faithful to Him will receive cities in their place, in accord with the work they have accomplished in His Name.

The time of our visitation is upon us; let us not be blind to its approach. As Jerusalem was crushed to the ground, so shall all this world be, without "one stone upon another." Do not cause your Savior to weep over your fate, but hear Him as He enters into your gates, as He preaches and teaches and even lays down His life for your sake – it *is* for souls such as your own that He has come, that He has taken this Cross upon Himself.

As Jesus approached the Mount of Olives (the place He will begin His Passion), "the whole multitude of His disciples began to praise God aloud with joy for all the mighty deeds they had seen." They could not remain silent, or even the stones would cry out for joy! How tremendous is His presence among us, He upon whom glory rests. But forget not what lies before Him, for His glory shall only be revealed in His death.

> O Lord, all you would bring into your holy way;
> our poor souls you ever venture to save.
> Enter into our corrupt houses,
> our polluted temples,
> and cleanse and purify us by your words and deeds,
> that we might serve you well
> and find a place at your table.

Chapter 20 – Persecution Rises

How well the Lord answers all questions – how well He reveals that He is Lord. And how true it is that this cornerstone rejected by the builders shall crush all rebellious against His authority. And none can answer Him.

The persecution against the Christ heats up as He teaches in the temple area, now only days from His death. His power the chief priests and scribes would dearly love to destroy, but their every effort is thwarted as each challenge is met and only serves to reveal further the greatness of Jesus and increase the people's awe in the presence of the Son of God.

There are those who would not see the Jewish leadership crushed, but what can be done? He is roundly rejected and there must be men who will stand in His stead once He is gone. There must ever be disciples to declare His resurrection, to declare that He is Lord and that His enemies have been made His footstool.

This only Son is not of human origin, but heavenly (note how He answers the elders' initial question about His authority in *His* question about David); and it is not to human praise He leads us, but divine. And only those who set their hearts on the things of heaven know Him; only those who give God His due receive the Son of Man. (And only these shall live again.)

> David calls Him "Lord",
> and we echo the blessed king's cry:
> O Lord, let us hear your Good News.
> You have come to find fruit with us
> and have died at the hands of those
> who would take your Sonship away.
> Let us not be among them
> but give our very souls to you.
> No questions have we to pose –
> only let us hear your Word.

Luke

Chapter 21 – Signs of the End

"Be vigilant at all times and pray that you have the strength to escape the tribulations that are imminent and to stand before the Son of Man." This is the bottom line of this chapter in which Jesus speaks openly of the "awesome sights and mighty signs [that] will come from the sky," "of wars and insurrections," of "powerful earthquakes, famines, and plagues," of "the roaring of the sea and its waves," and of the severe persecution all His disciples will face. He tells us many will "die of fright in anticipation of what is coming upon the world," but at the time of these signs we should "stand erect and raise [our] heads because [our] redemption is at hand."

"Jerusalem will be trampled underfoot by the Gentiles until the times of the Gentiles are fulfilled." But though our adversaries be given power to bring desolation to all the land, the Lord is with His faithful who give witness to Him; though some of us be put to death and all will be hated because of the Name's sake, "not a hair on [our] head will be destroyed." If we remain vigilant, we will only rejoice on the Day the powers that be are shaken.

"A terrible calamity will come upon the earth and a wrathful judgment upon this people"; but if we are like those who would "get up early each morning to listen to [Jesus] in the temple area" (despite the horrors His words portend), if we are as humble and generous with our lives as the poor widow whose story opens this chapter, then we shall have no fear even at the end of the world and our own lives. For we will know that the Lord is an unshakable refuge in any tribulation or trial.

> Listen attentively to His words, brothers and sisters;
> thirst for His voice before sunrise.
> Let your heart be led by the Spirit of God,
> and He will guide you through any darkness.
> And His punishment you shall escape
> if you allow Him to speak through you.
> O Lord, let our lives be lived in you;
> let all our days come to completion
> in your holy presence.

Chapters of the Gospels

Chapter 22 - Betrayed

The Passover nears and the chief priests and scribes look for a chance to kill the Christ, but they must get Him away from the people, who hang upon His words. Then Judas comes forward to answer their prayers, in timely fashion. ("The Son of Man indeed goes as it has been determined; but woe to that man by whom He is betrayed.")

Peter and John make preparation for the Passover meal in "the large upper room that is furnished" for the event; and to the table Jesus comes, to eat His Last Supper as He has eagerly desired, before He suffers. And the fruit of this table will sustain us till the end of time.

Here in Luke, after the Supper we find the argument breaking out among the apostles "about which of them should be regarded as the greatest." The Lord corrects their threatening vanity, but also confirms that He confers on them a kingdom, where they "will sit on thrones judging the twelve tribes of Israel." Indeed, these Twelve will be sifted like wheat, but they shall turn back, strengthened by Peter their leader.

Now they will be "counted among the wicked"; now they will all sleep while the Savior sweats drops of blood; now they will all flee Him as Judas betrays Him... and Peter will deny Him three times. Now He will stand alone, struck by the soldiers and declaring His divinity before the Sanhedrin – now He alone will be condemned to die. But soon the apostles will follow along the bloodied path Jesus marks out for all.

Yes, the time has come, the hour of the power of darkness. It has been ordained that He must suffer, and now the way of the Cross begins...

> O Lord, you go as you must;
> you suffer as your love requires.
> But when we weep as you look into our eyes,
> when we wake from slumbering through your agony,
> let us turn again to you
> and be strong in walking your way.
> Let your sacrifice bear fruit in the kingdom.

Luke

Chapter 23 – Condemned to Death

The voices of the people prevail upon Pilate, and he consents to their killing the Son of God.

He is the Messiah, no doubt. He is innocent and righteous as no other man, yet for this He is condemned – for His goodness He is crucified.

And not only crucified but treated shamefully, mocked and made to play the fool. By Herod and his soldiers, by the rulers of the Jews and all the people, He is taunted to reveal His kingship. But to only one does He listen and answer, only to the thief beside Him on the Cross, who steals Jesus' heart by recognizing his Savior's innocence and begging He remember his condemned soul. This man is with the Lord in Paradise.

To the lamenting women Jesus also speaks, telling them not to weep for Him. For it is they and their children who will suffer in a world turned cold to truth and love. And we would be hard-pressed to find a greater fulfillment of Jesus' words, "The days are coming when people will say, 'Blessed are the barren, the wombs that never bore and the breasts that never nursed,'" than in this age of the idols of abortion and contraception. Is it not most descriptive of this culture of death that men cry "to the mountains, 'Fall upon us!' and to the hills, 'Cover us!'" abandoning all hope of redemption? O how Rachel weeps in our day!

"This is the King of the Jews." This is He who suffers and dies for all mankind. Do we return home beating our breasts at His unrighteous death and our own participation therein? Are we "awaiting the kingdom of God" like Joseph of Arimathea, or seeking the tomb where His body rests (on this holiest Sabbath) and preparing Him spices as the women who have watched from a distance? How can we turn our hearts from what has happened to our Brother!

> O Lord, let repentance fill our souls
> as it has the thief upon the cross
> and all those aghast at the treatment you suffer.
> The little we can do to help you this day
> let us not hesitate to accomplish.
> We pray to be on the side of right

Chapters of the Gospels

    that we might meet you in Paradise
    with all who turn from their sin
    toward your blessed light.

Chapter 24 – The Third Day

    The third day. It seems His disciples did not remember "the third day." So overwhelmed by His death are they that only with great difficulty and great amazement are they able to recognize the Lord's risen presence.

    Indeed, "the Son of Man [had to] be handed over to sinners and be crucified, and rise on the third day." This teaching comes from the angels to the women at the tomb and from Jesus' own mouth to His disciples, on the road to Emmaus and in the room where they are all gathered.

    Yes, Luke tells us greatly in this chapter how the Lord "opened their minds to understand the Scriptures," expounding twice all that referred to Him, "beginning with Moses and all the prophets." It had been written for generations, plain for all to see, but only now as the risen Messiah speaks do our hearts burn so within us at the truth – for now the truth has been fulfilled.

    And how evident is the essence of holy Catholic Mass in these final passages of St. Luke. How we find the Liturgy of the Word and the Liturgy of the Eucharist presented. Particularly on the road to Emmaus, Scripture is opened to the faithful soul, then in the breaking of the bread Jesus is made known. And in the room again the Word is revealed... and here, too, Jesus eats. Then He blesses His disciples outside the city, before departing to heaven.

    He comes in peace and goes in peace. And peace He leaves with each of us. But we must believe, and in great joy praise the Lord for His blessings.

    You are risen, O Lord!
    You are not here
    in the cold stone of this world.
    Yet you are with us

and remain ever present
by the power of the Holy Spirit.
May we come to be where your body now sits,
eating the food of heaven.
Let us be "clothed with power from on high"
as we declare your glory to all.

Chapters of the Gospels

IV. The Gospel of John

Chapters of the Gospels

Chapter 1 – Word Made Flesh

The testimony of the great Evangelist John, beloved disciple of the Lord, begins. And with what humble, loving authority he speaks of the Word made flesh, of the Son of God. With the voice as of an angel, the Spirit indelibly upon him, he tells us of our Savior.

The Son is from the beginning. "All things came to be through Him." He is the light to which the Baptist testifies, the light of all men. In Him we see the Father's glory, for He is "full of grace and truth," and is ever at the Father's side.

John the Baptist is not the light, but has come to make straight the way of the light, the way of the Lord. Though none recognize the Lamb of God in our midst, and even the Baptist is blind to Him till the Spirit descends upon and remains with Him, yet now as he did not hesitate to state that *he* was *not* the Messiah, so he does not fail to proclaim openly that *Jesus is* the Christ, the Son of God.

May all souls accept Him and so find power to become children of God, even as the first disciples do. Here in John's first chapter, it is the Baptist who directs two of his own disciples toward the Lamb of God, and these bring others with them, as the Twelve begin to gather around their Master.

The Evangelist tells us that Andrew is one of the first two who come to Jesus, but, in typically humble manner, does not mention himself as the second of the Baptist's disciples led to the Lamb*. Nor does he mention his presumed call of his brother James, but only states that Andrew "first found his own brother Simon." Again, this is typical of the Lord's beloved apostle, who does not reveal his identity till the end of his testimony.

We hear also of Philip's call, and of his finding Nathanael; and already Nathanael, the true Israelite in whom is no guile, declares Jesus Son of God and King of Israel. (Great belief in the Lord's true nature is evident even here at the start of His ministry.)

Come to the Light revealed in John's Gospel, and see "the angels of God ascending and descending on the Son of Man."

---

* This second disciple – elsewhere "the one whom Jesus loved", "another disciple", "the other disciple" – is traditionally John, Son of Zebedee, the Evangelist himself. We hold to that traditional understanding throughout this writing.

> Glory to you, Lord Jesus Christ!
> and blessings upon your holy apostles.
> Send forth your word to the ends of the earth
> by the power of the Holy Spirit.
> Let our ears be open to the testimony
> of your beloved apostle.

<u>Chapter 2</u> – The True Temple

The signs Jesus performs begin to inspire belief in His disciples and the people in general. But on what shaky ground this faith can rest – the Lord knows what is in man.

Two events, the wedding at Cana and Jesus' cleansing of the temple, are recounted by John in this particularly short chapter of only twenty-five verses. At the wedding at Cana, the Lord changes the water into wine, answering His Mother's plea for sympathy toward the feast and the bride and groom. Though He expresses question regarding her request, here at her prompting the Christ indeed begins to reveal Himself.

One wonders if the Lord did not *need* His Mother's petition, her approval of His mission (which He might have started on His own at twelve years of age), in order to begin His ministry – much as He needs us to ask, to allow Him to enter our lives, in order to bring healing, in order to accomplish the salvation He has been called to fulfill in every soul. Is not His Mother the symbol of us all, of the Lord's blessed Church, His holy Temple?

Let us pray she continue to intercede and we continue to seek her intercession, desiring always that the will of the Father be done in us through His Son and by the power of the Holy Spirit. It is only this that will save us from what is inside our hearts, from the evil all around.

The evil all around, our Savior would purge from us and from our midst – and especially from God's holy Temple. And so, even with a whip of cords does He drive out those who pollute His Father's House. The hand of mammon has no place in the Church of God or in our souls, and so with zeal the Son of Man comes to purify both.

Chapters of the Gospels

There is no other way we shall be prepared for the true Temple that is built in three days.

All must make their home in the Body of Jesus, in Christ the Lord. He alone is the true Temple, and in Him alone do we truly feast in blessed joy. The wine He brings will endure forever, and ever surpass any vine of the earth. Remember, my brother, my sister, that He has been raised from the dead; the feast of the Passover has been fulfilled and we must now enter the Promised Land.

> In your presence alone do we dance and sing, O Lord,
> for any other celebration will ring hollow;
> no other feast can endure.
> You are the Temple wherein we pray –
> make our lips and our hearts holy,
> that we might worthily declare your Name.
> O let our faith in you be true!

Chapter 3 – His Way of Blood

Jesus comes from heaven and is above all. He testifies to what He has seen and heard, but "no one accepts His testimony." How can any? How can Nicodemus know what the Christ means when He tells him he "must be born from above" if the Son of Man has not been lifted up yet for all eyes to see the love of God displayed upon the Cross. He who has seen, knows; he who has witnessed His sacrifice for our sins realizes what it is to be of heaven and the way to get there – but he to whom the Cross has not yet been revealed will ever remain blind to the kingdom of God.

Jesus alone is the way and the truth and the life, and only following in His path of self-offering will any soul know what it is to be of the Spirit and find himself in heaven.

We now are not like Nicodemus then. We are more blessed than the disciples of John the Baptist, or even the Lord's own apostles at this time. For we have seen the Christ upon the Cross; we have heard and believed in the love God has shown to man, and so the call to be born of the Spirit no longer amazes our souls.

But this grace we must cherish with all our hearts. His way of blood we must remember and ever bring our deeds into the light, that we might ever be purified, that we might forever with Him remain. We know the Savior's testimony is true: let us not doubt but fly humbly to His presence this day.

The leaders of the people knew that He had come from God because He did the works of God. But the love of God was not in them. Let the love of God be foremost in our minds; let it lead us into all truth, and we will prove ourselves children of the Lord Most High.

> Spirit of God, descend upon us this day;
> renew us in the Father's grace each moment,
> that the sacrifice of the Son
> will be fulfilled in us
> and we will dwell eternally
> in heaven.

Chapter 4 – Coming to Faith

A Samaritan woman and many of her town, and a royal official and his whole household, come to faith in Jesus as the Savior of the world, even as His own disciples struggle in the flesh to understand His words.

The account of the Samaritan woman at Jacob's well is a remarkable one. Notice how the Lord leads from the flesh to the Spirit of God this woman foreign to the promise of the Jews. As John's description unfolds, first the woman is thoroughly befuddled, not only because a Jewish man is speaking to her, but because He is speaking of "living water." The water from the well is all she knows, and she makes this clear by her ignorant responses to Jesus' call.

But then our Lord speaks to her heart, revealing her deepest sins. He addresses her flesh and her failures therein – living unlawfully with men who are not her true husband. Her honesty and the Prophet's wisdom enlighten her mind, and here she begins to turn from the flesh to a desire for the Holy One.

She next begins to speak of the worship of God, and then of the Messiah that is to come. She indeed begins to hear and understand

Jesus' words that "God is Spirit," and her heart is aflame with a burgeoning faith in Him as the Anointed One. As she goes off to her townspeople, she has already heard that the One speaking with her is the Christ. She has drunk from the spiritual font.

But the only nourishment the disciples can see is the bread that is in their hands; and when Jesus says He has already eaten, how difficult the fruits of the Spirit, the work of the Father that produces food for souls and feeds even the bearer, are for them to comprehend. (Perhaps as the Samaritans come to faith more and more, the Lord's disciples also begin to enter His light.)

Then another Gentile comes to the faith before the eyes of the disciples. So intent is he on saving his ailing son that this royal official bows to the Kingship of Christ and trusts that the Word He offers is truth. From the Lord he departs with conviction that his son will be healed. When it is proven that the word of Jesus has indeed saved the boy from death, all those under his roof are also saved, as they come to believe in the One God has sent.

Witnessing these faithless peoples come to our own Lord and Savior cannot but cause us to question the strength of our own convictions, we who are of His native place, His native Church. Are we still in the flesh, or have we come to the Spirit?

> O Lord, instill your Word deeply in our souls,
> that our spirits might be alive to you
> and our hearts moved to proclaim your glory.
> Let our flesh prove no barrier to our faith
> in you who come to our table each day.

Chapter 5 – Son of God

Jesus is equal to God, is God. For this He is persecuted; because of this He must defend Himself, though His words fall on deaf ears.

Yes, Jesus offends against the Sabbath again, according to the Jewish leaders, by healing the sick man; and again He is called to task for such work. But it is for what these consider blasphemy that the Lord is truly persecuted. He tells the leading Jews that the Father never ceases to work, to give and maintain life in all His creatures,

John

and so neither does the Son cease to do good. Thus He indeed equates Himself to the God who rules all... and this is too much for these souls to hear. This man is claiming to be the Christ!

And though He has many witnesses to His glory – from the writings of Moses and all Scripture to the testimony of John the Baptist to His own works and even the Word of the Father Himself – still they deny His goodness and His power, and plug their ears against His teaching.

But it is so, that the Father loves the Son and gives everything over to Him, including all judgment. It is so, that the Day will soon come (and is already here) when the dead lying in their tombs will hear the voice of the Son of God and come forth either to eternal life or to condemnation. It is so, that on that Day His majesty none will be able to deny.

As He heals the man ill thirty-eight years, immediately, with but a word, so He can make each of us well. But we must never turn from Him to sin, and we must never seek the glory that comes from man but only the glory of heaven – or we will fall back again.

>Only through you is the Father's will done, Lord Jesus.
>Only you are the way and the truth;
>only you give life
>and take it away,
>for only you are blessed by God.
>Let us see the works you do
>and so be amazed,
>and so come to faith –
>let the love of God remain in us
>until your return.

Chapter 6 – Eat His Body

The Bread of Life and the bread that merely feeds the flesh. The food that endures for eternal life and the food that perishes. Though Jesus sees the need for and provides the latter, it is the former He has been sent from Heaven to give to men; it is the former He Himself is.

Chapters of the Gospels

Jesus feeds the five thousand, a loaf of bread for each thousand men… with an abundance left over. Is this not a sign that He is the Son of God? Does it not cause the people to cry out that He is the Prophet and to desire Him as their king? But a king of this earth He has not come to be, caring but for the needs of the body; water He can walk upon, but King of Heaven He is primarily, and only those with hearts seeking heavenly things are drawn by the Father to Him. The rest shall perish in their ignorance, though they have enough food to eat.

His flesh alone is "true food," and His blood "true drink." The living God resides in none who do not come to the Christ to eat His flesh and drink His blood. He makes clear that those who doubt His call to life, those who cannot accept this hard saying, will not come to the heavenly kingdom. They will be led by their bellies to abandon, if not betray Him.

But we must be "taught by God." We must have the words of everlasting life breathing in our souls; and, yes, we must eat His body and drink His blood. We must come to the table He prepares to nourish us here in our journey on earth.

The Lord looks up and sees our needs. He wishes to feed us with His own body. Do not accuse Him of cannibalism or fail to make real the call upon which hinges your eternal salvation. Come to Him, my brother, my sister. Come to Him and remain in Him who gives us this bread always, who withholds His very body and blood from no soul who comes to Him in faith, believing in Him who is the life-giving Bread from heaven.

Do you know His heavenly Father? Then you will come to Him even this day, without hesitation, with no doubt of His Word to trouble your soul.

> O Lord, let us never turn away from you;
> let us never question your origins
> or your words of life.
> Eternally let us remain with you
> who feed us with the spiritual Bread
> we eat at your table each day.
> Thank you for coming to us across the waters
> and feeding us so generously.
> In you we come to the shore we seek.

Chapter 7 – Jesus' Origins

"Stop judging by appearances, but judge justly." Indeed it is only by appearances that all souls judge the Lord at this time, for the Spirit has not yet come to enlighten their minds, nor to manifest His glory. And so, blindly do the people grope, trying to understand this remarkable Person among them.

There is great preoccupation with the Christ's human origins in this chapter, and it serves as the primary obstacle to belief in Him as the Messiah. His own brothers, those of Galilee, the town in which the Son was raised, are the epitome of the problem, of the blindness. They themselves do not believe in Him. They have grown up with Him, they have seen and been with Him all their lives, and so they cannot see beyond His human side. He seems but a man to them, and how can a man be God?

The crowds, who seem upon belief in Him for the signs He performs and the authority with which He speaks (though into His divinity they cannot see), also stumble at this question, stating, "We know where He is from. When the Messiah comes, no one will know where He is from"; and, "Does not Scripture say that the Messiah will be of David's family and come from Bethlehem?" As the Pharisees emphasize to Nicodemus, "Look and see that no prophet arises from Galilee."

Jesus' origins are hidden from all their eyes. Not only are they ignorant of His conception by the Holy Spirit and so His heavenly origins, but they are even unaware that He was not born in Galilee; it is presumed He is Galilean because of the time He has spent there since His youth, but in truth He *was* born in Bethlehem and *is* of the line of David. (The Lord God uses this human blindness to keep souls blind to the spiritual vision of the Son's divinity, which would only serve to blind them forever… without the Spirit as they stand.)

But Jesus does call to the people. He would lead them to what they cannot comprehend at this time but will later be able to understand. Indeed, none can follow where He goes now, but when the Spirit comes, all will be known. Till then there is division among and within all souls, and a seeking to grasp what is kept from their reach by those who would find the glory of God.

O Lord, let your living water flow through us today.
You have died and risen,
and your Spirit has come.
We have no excuse for our blindness
in this time.
All is now revealed to those who seek you
with a whole heart.
Let any confusion be banished from our midst.

Chapter 8 – Sins to Light

Those who are of lies and sin do not know Him, for He is of the truth and God and these are from the world and the devil.

It is right to ask what Moses would say, to question who is a son of Abraham, for with the Lawgiver and the Patriarch there is truth; there is the finger of God at work, be it to engrave His commands in stone or to produce offspring unto the Promised Land. But Jesus is before any patriarch or prophet – He is the Son of God, the Great I AM come into our midst.

And though He speaks only truth and cannot be gainsaid by any, though He does the works of the Father and proves Himself the true Son, yet those who claim Abraham as their father deride the Son of Man as a Samaritan and one possessed by the devil – yet they would stone Him to death as an adulterer.

But there is no adultery in His speech; there is only love in all His deeds. And when He is lifted up on the Cross, all shall indeed see that He is the Great I AM. (How could one then deny the love of the Father so perfectly at work in Him?)

But for now those who do not believe cannot bear being called illegitimate, cannot face the sins that are upon every human being's hands. They know they are with sin, for when confronted by the Lord to throw the first stone if they be clean, each one turns away. Yet when He speaks of their sins openly in the light only He brings, in the light only He is, pride and anger but build up in them.

He is well able to judge your soul, my brother, my sister. Take His Word as a gift that will set you free. For as long as you turn from the truth He speaks, as long as you fail to recognize your own illegitimacy, so long will your heart harden, until you die in your sins.

The light of Christ has come to save humanity – keep His Word and you will not see death.

> O Lord, let us not belong to this world,
> but follow rather where you lead –
> beyond the veil of this flesh
> and the condemnation we inherit
> to redemption with you at the Father's right hand.
> Your glory may we know;
> Abraham's children in faith let us be,
> rejoicing with him to see your Day
> as we humble ourselves in the dust of this earth.

Chapter 9 – The Man Born Blind

As long as we say, "We see," we are blind; but if we admit our blindness, the Lord will take our sin away.

It is sin that blinds us, no doubt, though it is not physical blindness about which we should be concerned; it is not our eyes which are attacked by the ravages of sin, but rather our souls. The blinding of our minds to spiritual matters is what we should most fear – from this, only repentance will save us.

The man born blind is physically healed. He is set free from his crippling disability. This is good; all healing is in the hands of God, and only He can work such wonders. But the man's eyes are not at the heart of this account (which occupies this entire chapter) – the crux of the matter is the blindness of the Pharisees to God and His Son, to the goodness of the Lord and the mercy He would share with all.

Though a real man really healed, the man is primarily a symbol. Though this sign Jesus performs serves as proof that He is the Messiah, what is more important is that *He is the Messiah* and that every soul must come to Him and believe in Him... and so avoid sin. To this the man himself witnesses. Jesus He comes to see as the Son

Chapters of the Gospels

of Man, and readily declares His goodness to all. Here is the true healing.

Jesus does the works of God while it is still day, and all His followers must do the same. We are all called to feed the hungry and set captives free from their blindness to sin. While there is light, while we have the Lord with us, we must work. Indeed, "night is coming when no one can work," when the hand of God shall accomplish all, bringing this world to a close… but while it is day, let us carry Christ's light forth.

He who is of sin can neither heal nor be healed. Let us turn from our sin to the One who has no sin and, unashamed and unafraid of the consequences, proclaim His truth before all.

> You give wisdom to the simple soul, O Lord;
> you alone open the eyes of all men.
> Let us turn from our pride and selfishness
> and embrace your healing touch upon our hearts.
> Loose our tongues to speak your praise
> even as you bring light to our minds.

Chapter 10 – The Good Shepherd

Jesus is "the One whom the Father has consecrated and sent into the world." He Himself tells us this plainly. But who believes that "the Father is in [Him] and [He] in the Father"? Who recognizes His voice and follows Him to eternal life? Who holds Him firmly as the Good Shepherd who lays down His life for the sheep?

The Jews, those who have the promise of His coming and are the first to hear His voice, struggle to believe that this Jesus is the Messiah. Their Scripture testifies to the One who will come and give them life abundantly, who will perform great works in their midst to reveal the Father's glory… Yet when He comes among them performing such signs and offering such life, their human nature cannot open to His divinity.

Some are thieves and robbers, certainly. Others are but hired hands with little concern for the sheep in their care. But how can *anyone* embrace fully the revelation the Christ brings, the revelation the Christ *is*, not only for the flock of His chosen but for all men?

Do not think you would have so soon listened to His voice calling your name in purity and in light. Do not imagine that you would *never* have picked up a rock to stone Him. Know that you would have been blessed if among those who simply "began to believe in Him." For even now how strong is your faith?

Still we question the Lord and His followers, looking for a way to accuse them of blasphemy, our hearts hardened against what is plain to our eyes. Though we receive the fruit of His works on a daily basis, though we would perish if He withheld His Word from us even for an hour, yet what division remains!

He is the Christ. He has been sent by the Father. He and the Father are one, and only in their love do we find the Spirit. Be held in the hand of the Lord.

> O Good Shepherd, your sheep thirst for your voice;
> speak to our hearts and lead us forth
> in the will of the Father.
> Apart from you, we would perish,
> but you lay down your life
> that we might live forever.
> Help our unbelief;
> let us enter and remain in your fold.

Chapter 11 – Lazarus

"Untie him and let him go," Jesus says of the risen Lazarus; and this He says to all souls wrapped in the burial bands of sin, entombed in the darkness of death, a death that hangs above all our heads like a cloud poised to fall.

Do not fear the bonds of death; they have no strength where the Savior reigns. But believe He is the Messiah, the Son of God, and you will know the resurrection and the life, and you will never die.

These are the Lord's own words, spoken to Martha (who stands in our stead), anxious about her brother's death. They are for every soul to hear and heed – all must believe that Jesus is the Christ, with power over even death.

The Lord knows we are weak; He knows how we weep. He knows we are slow to believe – He knows with what difficulty we come to recognize His glory. But He would have us come into His light. So He allows the one whom He loves, His dear friend Lazarus, to die.

Scripture tells us explicitly that because Jesus loved Lazarus, "when He heard that he was ill, He remained for two days in the place where He was." He did not rush to his side, as one would naturally be inclined, but stayed apart and let His friend's sickness take its course.

Certainly He could have saved him, as both Martha and Mary attest. Certainly He could have "done something so that this man would not have died," as the crowds comment. But this death He permits to take place that a greater good might come of it, indeed, not only because He loves Lazarus and would have him symbolically precede Himself to the gates of death and the nether world – from whose grasp he shall be snatched away – but because He loves us all and would have us witness what little mastery death has over the Son of Man.

"Lazarus has died. And I am glad for you that I was not there, that you may believe." These are the Savior's words to His disciples. Hear them and know how He cares for you, how He will rescue you, too.

There is only one Man who dies for all the people, "that the whole nation might not perish." He alone suffers death, for the sake of every soul. The Passover Lamb will soon be sacrificed.

> O Lord, you are our Redeemer,
> saving us from the snares of sin and death,
> calling us out of our tombs.
> The tomb you alone shall occupy
> to bring your light even there,
> that in this dark cave none should remain
> but come to resurrection and eternal life.
> From the Cross you weep for us
> to receive the love you offer…
> Come to us on the third day.

John

Chapter 12 – Royal Welcome

He is the light that has come into the world to save all souls from darkness; and how brightly that light does shine as the time draws nigh for the ruler of this world, the prince of darkness, to be cast out by the death of the only Son.

John has told us in the previous chapter that everyone was looking to see if Jesus would come to the Passover feast, for the chief priests and Pharisees had designs to arrest Him. Yet here He not only comes to the feast, but is recognized and praised by all as the King of Israel! A royal welcome is given Him as He rides into Jerusalem on the colt of an ass.

Even the Greeks among them seek out this Jesus: all the world is drawn to His presence. And so, the Lord knows it is time now for Him to fall to the ground, to be planted in the earth like a grain of wheat that He might produce abundant fruit – His mission having been fulfilled, He must die, that His disciples might carry His Word to the ends of the earth. (Walk in His light this day.)

A few interesting details on these penultimate events John provides. Here Lazarus is at table with Jesus at the supper before His entry into Jerusalem. Here Mary is specified as the woman who anoints Him (His feet rather than His head). Here, too, Judas is named as the sole disciple who disputes such extravagant anointing, and his reason is given – he held the purse and was a thief.

The Lord's recent raising of Lazarus takes a primary place in the events, both as a cause of the outpouring of praise among the people and, thus, a further reason for the chief priests to desire His death (as well as the death of Lazarus himself).

John also informs us of how even the disciples were blind at the time to the manner in which Scripture was being fulfilled before their eyes. Only later would they realize things such as Zechariah's prophecy of their King coming to them mounted on an ass's colt had been accomplished. For, as John emphasizes once more and throughout this chapter, even those who seem to believe, who shout His Name or sense His glory in their hearts, do not come into His light, do not understand the kind of glory that awaits Him and His followers.

Chapters of the Gospels

As the Father Himself declares, even to the ears of the people, His Name will be glorified... but, again, only His being lifted up on a cross will reveal that glory to our eyes.

> O Lord, let us indeed walk in your light;
> let us not be afraid to acknowledge you openly
> and be as those whom you have sent.
> Let us join you in revealing the Father's glory
> in the lives we lead
> and the death we embrace as your servants.

Chapter 13 – Night Falls

Jesus' preparation of His apostles for His departure by His washing of their feet and exhorting them to love one another is framed by the betrayal of Judas, who acts as the instrument to bring about His death.

Three times the Lord speaks of Judas' betrayal in this chapter: in saying that not all of His apostles are clean, in declaring that one of those who eats with Him will raise his heel against Him... and then in specifically pointing to Judas. And John mentions it another time at the beginning of the chapter, to illustrate that Jesus' "hour had come to pass from this world to the Father."

Before He goes, though, and before Judas leaves to complete the plot that has been hatched, our Lord and Master, "fully aware that the Father had put everything into His power and that He had come from God and was returning to God," indeed stoops down to wash the feet of His apostles, even as the meanest slave. He who is exalted above all and teaches all, here imparts His greatest lesson, of humility and service to others. (In what contrast does it stand to the devil's sin – and Judas' sin – of pride and betrayal.)

He is the great I AM and His model of sacrifice we must follow. We too must lay down our lives as has our Teacher, or we shall not be glorified with Him – or we shall never follow Him into the Father's loving arms.

Jesus is troubled deeply by Judas' betrayal, but there are others that increase the impending darkness. Indeed, when the traitorous apostle leaves, we are told, "It was night," as if all light flees the room as the Cross of Christ is prepared... but it is also indicated that His own Rock, the first among the Twelve, will add to the darkness of the night by his denial of the Lord, despite the declaration of his readiness to die for Him; and the other apostles (and you and I) will quickly follow Peter.

> Wash my feet, O Lord,
> that they might not tread wicked paths
> in opposition to you.
> Though darkness fall all about us, too,
> let us not forget that you are with us,
> but follow by love where you lead.

Chapter 14 – The Spirit's Consolation

Looking upon Him, we see the Father. Keeping His commands, we come to Him in the Spirit. He who has kept the commands of His Father, He upon whom the Spirit rests, is preparing a place for those who love Him: "Do not let your hearts be troubled." Have faith in the Lord.

The consolation of the Spirit is already present in the words Jesus speaks to His apostles here at the Last Supper. He knows He is going to the Father and is resolved to walk the way of truth set before Him; but He is concerned that His brothers not be anxious about His death, for He doesn't leave us.

Closer indeed to all our souls does Jesus come now that He is united more perfectly with the Father in heaven. He is not distant from our hearts but present within them by the power of the Holy Spirit. The Spirit, who is the love of the Father and the Son, now finds great joy in their union... and so His love pours forth freely upon all who keep God's Word, upon all who, in turn, love.

Brothers and sisters, our place will be well set by our holy Lord, and He will come back for us to grant what He has prepared. Indeed, we will be united with Him in the Father by the power of the Holy Spirit – the love of the Trinity will be our own.

A more marvelous gift we could not imagine or find on our own, so do not be afraid, though death does come; there is a kingdom without end. Arise, let us be going.

> Your peace leave with us, dear Lord,
> in this troubled place.
> Let our hearts be set on your kingdom
> and we shall not fear.
> With the Father in heaven let us ever remain,
> with you and by the Holy Spirit...
> We commend our spirits into your hands.

<u>Chapter 15</u> – Preparation by Persecution

The Lord speaks His Word unto us and we are pruned, and we are purified to bear fruit. Let His Word, His commandment to love, remain in you; endure the persecution, the purification that must follow, and you will remain ever in Him, doing the works of the Father.

The Word, His works, love, truth, persecution, and joy, all coincide in the teaching of Jesus, and in the laying down of His life. His Word He speaks, the Father's work He does... and what is this Word, and what is this work, but the commandment to love and the fruit of a holy life?

And how do we love except by laying down our lives, by enduring all trials in His Name and so finding the joy of the new life to which He calls us, for which He has chosen us? And to what do we testify by our own words and works but that He is Truth and we must obey Him... and so share in His love?

It is from the world we are called: all that is of the world will be burned up in the fire. Hatred shall die, lies cannot survive – only that which is blessed by God is everlasting, and so we must be branches of the vine that is Jesus His Son.

Yes, we have been blessed to know Jesus and His Word. Keep that Word alive in you, meditating on His law day and night, and nothing will separate you from the kingdom of God.

> O Lord, let your Word of truth grow in us,
> enabling us to bear fruit each day
> in your love.
> The grace you offer take not from our hearts,
> but let us be your friends,
> testifying to your glory
> in this troubled world.

Chapter 16 – "You Will See Me"

"A little while and you will not see me, and again a little while and you shall."

Jesus is going to the Father, returning whence He came, now that His work is complete. This departure, and the terrible death He will have to endure, grieves the disciples… and it will cause them to flee His side, leaving Him alone as He is crucified.

But He does go to the Father and the Father is always with Him. And though the disciples themselves be in anguish now, they will rejoice when He rises; and though they suffer persecution in giving witness to Him, the Spirit will always be with them, turning their sorrow to joy.

We all must suffer for the sake of Christ; we must finish the work He has begun. And though the task at hand bring trial and persecution, though it be a cross we must bear, truly it is Jesus who carries our cross for us, by the power of the Spirit on high.

We must know the Spirit is upon us in all we do for the sake of the Lord. God does not leave us alone, Jesus is not far from any one of us, for His Spirit is at hand if we but seek His guidance.

Do not be afraid. And do not despair for your abandonment of Jesus. Believe now in Him and sin will flee. Know that He is with the Father and you will stand with Him. Leave the devil to be condemned – you are the offspring of Christ's sacrifice.

> Though we weep and mourn, be with us, Lord.
> Turn our hearts to the Spirit's care.
> He is with you and you with the Father,

and it is your desire that we be there, too.
Help us to conquer the world in your Name.

Chapter 17 – Prayer to the Father

Jesus' final words at the Last Supper are a prayer – all of them (this entire chapter) are addressed to His heavenly Father, asking that He be glorified, and His disciples with Him.

Jesus looks up to heaven throughout His prayer, allowing those who have been His closest followers to overhear this most intimate petitioning of the Father. And His concern for all who follow Him is evident, is that which prompts Him now to pray. He indeed is leaving the world, His hour has come, and His attention turns not to the suffering He is about to endure, but to the perseverance of His flock. And so He calls God's blessed protection down upon us.

O to be consecrated in His truth! O to be one in Him! O to share in the love of Father and Son all the days of our life! Have we truly believed that Jesus has come from the Father and returned to the Father? Do we realize how He watches over us even this day? Or do we still somehow belong to the world? Are we thus in some measure deaf to the Lord's words? Does the glory of eternal life therefore elude our grasp?

To understand His words we must open our hearts and lay down our lives in this world, as our Savior has done. We indeed remain in the world, but of the world we must never be. Of the love of God we must be born, and Jesus' words will be our refuge in any storm – and the Spirit will lead us home… and we will be one.

> O Father in heaven,
> fulfill the prayer of your only Son.
> Let Him be glorified now in you,
> and we be glorified, too, in Him.
> In your truth and your love
> let us make our home.

Chapter 18 – The Cock Crows

The cock crows, exposing our sin, crying it out in the middle of the night. And who can hide from the truth – that we are all sinners, that He is the Son of God? Come to this King and be redeemed, be you a governor or a humble maid.

How anxious Peter must have been, sitting in the courtyard with those who had arrested Jesus, those with whom he himself had fought. It is John who gets him inside the gate to the high priest's residence, and everyone knows John is one of the disciples – so mustn't this other one be a disciple as well? Didn't they see him in the garden? Didn't he cut off Malchus' ear?

But what can Peter do? The Lord has instructed him to put away his sword. He cannot break in on the trial and fight for the King of the Jews, and he cannot leave his Savior alone... so in this cold courtyard he remains, in neither place, nor where he is. And his enemies surround him; and he can't find a weapon to use. (It is, of course, the fire of the Holy Spirit he needs to warm himself by, and the Word of God should be his sword... but that hour has not yet come – though it shall; yes, it shall.)

And could Pilate be more nervous than now as he stands before a man whose power he cannot surmount, who by His truth reduces this world – this world in which Pilate is a prince – to dust? He recognizes the innocence of Jesus, in addition to His power (if not His divinity), but what can he do? The Jews will call for His death, and he has an office to fulfill?

Before the great I AM all fall to their faces; none can ignore the glory of God as it rests upon Jesus the Son. But He will allow Himself to be crucified, that He might draw us all from our sins.

> In the trial of the human court,
> Truth is condemned, O Lord;
> you are despised
> and your disciples cower in fear.
> Let this not be the end,
> but let your kingdom come
> in strength and majesty.

Chapter 19 – Behold Your King

"Behold the man!" – "the King of the Jews" – He who is scourged, He who is crowned with thorns, He who is raised upon a cross. "Behold your King!" brothers and sisters, Him whom we have crucified.

His garments are divided amongst us; lots are cast for His coat. He thirsts for us and gives us to His Blessed Mother… but we pierce His side to be sure He is dead.

A tomb is prepared for Him; it is ready at hand – this is the home we make for the Son of Man.

The women upon whose hearts the bitterness of His blood falls weep at the foot of the Cross, along with His beloved John. Will we find our place beside them? Will we come to worship our pummeled King? Or will fear and mockery take possession of our souls, and in this debacle we be lost?

The chief priests cry adamantly for His death; they disown their Messiah, their very Savior, in favor of the king of this world. His wounds leave them unmoved. And though a Gentile hand Him over, how can he be guiltier than these, upon whom no mere worldly power rests, but the word of God Himself?

But it is indeed each of us who must acknowledge our guilt in His blood being let. The mission He accomplishes nailed to the wood is to serve the salvation of every sinful soul – not the Jews alone.

> Only in death do we provide you perfume, Lord;
> while you walk amongst us,
> we do but turn away.
> Forgive the hardness of our hearts and minds,
> which would have indeed broken your bones
> if you would have allowed it.
> Now what can we do but wait
> and pray?

Chapter 20 – Peace Be With You

"Peace be with you." The Lord indeed comes, risen from the dead, to reassure His disciples, that we might "believe that [He] is the Messiah, the Son of God, and that through this belief [we] may have life in His Name" – that we might weep no more at His tomb.

The eyes of Mary Magdalene and Jesus' disciples see Him standing before themselves, and so they believe; and so Thomas, who had doubted the reports, falls to his knees and exclaims, "My Lord and my God!" before the Savior of all. John had come to belief upon gazing at the empty tomb, and Peter, too, found the Lord there among the discarded burial cloths. But all our hearts are not so quick to understand… and so the apostles witness so diligently.

And so John has written his Gospel for our sakes, that down through the ages what he ran to see that Easter morning might be known to the hearts of all who seek truth and light, of all who seek the Christ… that no poor soul might weep inconsolably anymore, but that the angels might minister well to Jesus' blessed disciples.

Rejoice in the presence of the Lord, brothers and sisters! His flesh is before us in the bread His priests consecrate, and our blindness is removed by their intercession in the sacrament of Reconciliation, instituted here in these pages of St. John. You have all you need to find the risen Lord. See Him, touch Him, and believe.

>Breathe upon us the Holy Spirit, Jesus,
>that we too might partake of your blessings.
>The holes we have made in your hands and your side
>now open up to eternal life.
>Let us worship you, O Risen God,
>that life might be ours in your Name.

Chapters of the Gospels
Chapter 21 – "Follow Me"

Jesus appears to the disciples at dawn by the sea. The scene is reminiscent of Luke's account of the call of these fishermen to follow the Lord: they have toiled all night in vain; Jesus asks them to make another cast; they catch an overwhelming number of fish... and He is recognized as the Lord.

In the morning light the disciples sit upon the shore and breakfast with the Lord. He awaits them with a charcoal fire and fish and bread. They enter into communion with Him, and when their meal is finished He speaks to Peter, asking the Rock of the Church of his love and entrusting His sheep into his care.

Here the definition of love is put forth: Does Peter love Jesus enough to die for Him and His lambs? If one loves, one is willing to sacrifice one's life: greater love has no man than this. Peter follows His Master, but John follows too, and Peter wonders what call the Lord has for this disciple, His beloved one. He seems to ask, in all humility, if John might not better serve as principal Shepherd of God, laying down his life for the flock – Is it not he who loves the most, who lies closest to Jesus' heart?

But each must go as the Lord calls. So Peter will indeed sacrifice his life as has the Christ, and the other disciples shall, too. But John will remain, proclaiming the Good News of Jesus we read till this day.

I pray you be evangelized by the Word of God and share in the meal had only in line with Peter, the head of the Church, ordained so by the risen Lord.

> O Lord, you know we love you;
> help us to lay down our lives.
> In your Word and in your Church
> let us make our home,
> that we might truly follow
> the way you call us this day.
> Feed us on our journey
> to your kingdom.

OTHER BOOKS by JAMES KURT

"TURN and Become like Children":
Refuting the Presumed Contradictions of the Jerusalem Bible
Old Testament Commentary –
A case study recounting the problems afflicting modern biblical scholarship
as exemplified in the JB. 188 pp. 2019.

"Into Your Hands...":
Distillation of the Letters of Fr. Jean-Pierre de Caussade –
Reflections of the profound counsel of Fr. De Caussade to embrace the Cross
and find the Lord's will (and joy) even in our greatest sufferings. 82 pp. 2019.

Prayers to the Saints (Updated) –
A page of prayer to each saint on the General Roman Calendar
for the United States. 237 pp. 2019 (original 2007). w/ imprimatur.

Our Daily Bread:
Exposition of the Readings of Catholic Mass –
A page of writing for every Mass of the liturgical calendar for the Roman Rite;
reflections drawn from the readings. 727 pp. 2004. w/ imprimatur.
Our Daily Bread: Lent – 86 pp. 2019. w/ imprimatur.

Remembrance of Things Present –
A mystical work seeking the presence of the LORD in the moment,
where He dwells at all times. 100 pp. 2018. w/ imprimatur.

Two Books: Paradox and the Christian Faith /
           Hippie Convert –
The apparent contradictions of the Faith are explained for those who seek wisdom;
and a member of the flower generation addresses true love and peace,
in poetic form. 238 pp. 2016. w/imprimatur.

Lines of Grace: Meditations on Verses of Holy Scripture,
The Stations of the Cross, and The Most Holy Rosary –
A Catholic devotional especially for the encouragement of the practice
of plenary indulgence. 195 pp. 2016.

Christian Vision of the Old Testament –
Synopsis and exhortation; faith-filled overview of all books of the Old Testament as
prefiguration of Jesus, with a focus on the prophetic nature of God's Word. 273
pp. 2013. w/ imprimatur.

Blessed Guilt: A Universal Conversion Story –
Extended parable on the life-giving repentance found in Jesus' blood;
vaguely autobiographical but without particulars.
119 pp. 2013. w/ imprimatur.

*The Most Holy Trinity
and the Four Corners of the Universe* –
A collection of writings on the Trinity and its reflection in Creation;
founded upon the Shema.   300 pp. 2008. w/ imprimatur.

YHWH: Order of the Divine NAME –
On the significance of the contemplative silence that is the NAME of God,
and its application to a spiritual life.   260 pp. 2008 (reprint 2019). w/ imprimatur.

Turn of the Jubilee Year: A Conversion Song –
Autobiographical depiction of vocation search through pilgrimage to Medjugorje
and stays at a hermitage or two.   230 pp. 2004.

Songs for Children of Light: Ten Albums of Lyrics –
A white on black conceptual work with simple drawings for each song.
150 pp. 2003.

silence in the city –
Short contemplative poems; moments of divine silence in the midst of city life.
148 pp. (74 pieces). 2003.

Author's Website:
www.writingsofjameskurt.org

Podcasting Site:
www.hermitinthecity.libsyn.com

www.ingramcontent.com/pod-product-compliance
Lightning Source LLC
Chambersburg PA
CBHW021114080526
44587CB00010B/520